W.H.O.L.E

Five Practical Steps to Wholeness in Spirit, Soul, and Body

LIFEWORK PRESS

W.H.O.L.E

Five Practical Steps to Wholeness
in Spirit, Soul, and Body

ARE YOU W.H.O.L.E?

GLORIA GODSON

LIFEWORK PRESS

W.H.O.L.E: 5 Practical Steps to Wholeness in Spirit, Soul and Body

LifeWork Ministries, Inc.
P. O. Box 56
Townsend, DE 19734

www.lifeworkministries.org
lifeworkministriesinc@gmail.com

LifeWork Press
© 2021 by Gloria Godson

All rights reserved solely by the author. No part of this book may be reproduced in any form without the permission of the author. For permission requests, contact author at lifeworkministriesinc@gmail.com.

Unless otherwise indicated, Scripture quotations taken from the Holy Bible, New Living Translation (NLT). Copyright ©1996, 2004, 2007 by Tyndale House Foundation. Used by permission of Tyndale House Publishers, Inc.

Scripture quotations taken from the New King James Version (NKJV)–*public domain*.

Printed in the United States of America.

ISBN: 978-5-3861-2092-4

**Dedicated
to
my Friend and Partner, Holy Spirit
and the men and women who have inspired
me on my journey to wholeness.**

CONTENTS

Introduction

Chapter 1—Wholeness...1
- i. W.H.O.L.E
- ii. Why is Wholeness so Important?
- iii. Un-Whole Connections
- iv. Becoming Whole
- v. The Devil's Identity Theft Strategy
- vi. Pathway to Victory
- vii. Codependency, the Relationship Lie
- viii. Is Jesus Enough for You?

Chapter 2— Well..34
- i. What is a Well Soul?
- ii. Whole People Take Charge of their Emotions
- iii. How Can You Have a Well Soul?
- iv. How to Break Curses and Demonic Covenants
- v. Enemies of Wellness

Chapter 3—Healthy..69
- i. Healthy Spirit
- ii. Healthy Soul
- iii. How to Cultivate a Healthy Soul
- iv. Deliverance from Oppression
- v. Personal Vows and How to Break Them
- vi. Healthy Conscience
- vii. Healthy Body
- viii. Healthy Attitude

Chapter 4—On-Fire 109
    i.   Where Did the Fire Go?
    ii.   God's Holiness
    iii.   The Zeal of the Lord
    iv.   Restoration of Holy Fire
    v.   The Power of a Personal Altar
    vi.   Fellowship of the Unashamed
    vii.   How to Successfully Engage This Season of Life
    viii. Invest in Eternity

Chapter 5—Loving 141
    i.   Love is the Greatest
    ii.   Biblical Love
    iii.   Loving Yourself
    iv.   Loving Others
    v.   Love Languages
    vi.   Sexuality and the Christian
    vii.   Why are Sexual Sins Worse Than Other Sins?
    viii. Soul Ties and Spiritual Orbits
    ix.   Social Media and the Quest for Love
    x.   Unequally Yoked

Chapter 6—Empowered 194
    i.   Who is the Holy Spirit?
    ii.   Empowered to Be
    iii.   Becoming Who You Are
    iv.   Empowered to Do
    v.   Empowered to Love
    vi.   Holy Spirit Baptism

Afterword 207

INTRODUCTION

Our world is flooded with fear, worry, and anxiety. National politics, wars, Covid 19 pandemic, social isolation, mammoth inflation, and economic uncertainty have stripped many people of hope for the future and confidence in their ability to cope. Loss, injustice, life circumstances, and disappointments compound these insecurities and turn them into limitations. Others struggle with low self-esteem, wrong self-definition, negative self-talk, misplaced identity, and wrong mindsets. God wants to heal and restore these broken areas of our lives! **God wants us to be whole.**

The Bible says in Job 5:18, that "God's hands make whole." What this means is that God has a personal commitment to your wholeness and takes a "hands on" approach to bringing it to pass. This approach is outlined in this book. God wants you to be Well, Healthy, On-fire, Loving and Empowered, and His hands are actively engaged, daily, in the good work of making you whole. Wholeness is both a process and a destination. This book provides a blueprint to guide you in your journey through the 5 steps to wholeness, enables a personal inventory of your progress, and provides a yard stick to measure your advancement towards that destination.

In the Bible, the word translated as WHOLE is also translated as well, save, deliver, restore, and heal. It is used by Jesus several times in His ministry. In every context, the word "whole" is used as an expression or manifestation of the love of God, and, Jesus repeatedly attributed wholeness to faith, and made the point that wholeness comes about as an exercise of faith. He said to the woman with the issue of blood, and to the one leper out of ten who came back to give thanks for his healing, "your faith has made you whole". This indicates that activating our faith in Christ is the key that unlocks wholeness in our lives.

Jesus is a package deal. The same package that delivered your salvation, also included your healing, financial provision, favor, and wholeness. Everything you need to live a godly life was included in your salvation package. Second Peter 1:3 says that everything we could ever need for life and godliness has already been deposited in us by God's divine power. This means that when we gave our lives to Christ, we received, through Christ, access to all of heaven's store house and limitless resources.

God has already provided wholeness for you in spirit, soul, and body. But you must know how to take God's provision and make it yours in reality. This book shows you how.

W.H.O.L.E

Five Practical Steps to Wholeness in Spirit, Soul, and Body

LIFEWORK PRESS

CHAPTER 1
WHOLENESS

Merriam Webster's dictionary defines "whole" as, "A thing that is complete in itself; all of something; entire; in an unbroken or undamaged state, in one piece, intact, entire, full, uncut, sum total, unity."

A whole person is a person who is complete in themselves and who they are in Christ, a person who is sufficient, entire, undivided, full, and in one piece. A whole person is a person of strength, dignity, unity, and grace. Whole people are men and women of tremendous worth who value themselves, own their personal value, and are confident in themselves, and their God. Whole people are free people who live interesting lives; lives that are free from self-pity, regret, desperation, depression, and low self-esteem. Whole people are men and women who make a choice daily to honor God, invest in the lives of others, and live an abundant life. They are men and women who act on purpose and with intentionality to impact their world, and transform the lives of people in their sphere of influence - their children, relatives, spouse, co-workers, friends, and so on. Whole people are men and women who are comfortable in their own skin, and live lives of purpose, passion and power.

> *Whole people are men and women of tremendous worth who value themselves, own their personal value, and are confident in themselves, and their God.*

Simply stated, a whole person is a person who does not have to look outside of themselves and Christ who lives in them, for their sense of self-worth, personal validation, confidence, affirmation, and wellbeing. They know that in Christ, they are enough! They are self-sufficient in Christ's sufficiency. Apostle Paul was whole! In Philippians 4:13 (AMP) he said, "I can do all things, which He has called me to do, through Him who strengthens and empowers me to fulfill His purpose. I am self-sufficient in Christ's sufficiency; I am ready for anything and equal to anything through Him who infuse me with inner strength and confident peace." What he is saying is that he finds his confidence, faith, strength, empowerment, purpose, peace, and wellbeing in Christ. He was whole.

W.H.O.L.E

Wholeness is not a reference to physical, mental, or emotional ability, or disability. W.H.O.L.E stands for:

W – WELL
H – HEALTHY
O – ON-FIRE
L – LOVING
E – EMPOWERED

I am convinced beyond any doubt that a person cannot be whole if they are not well, healthy, on-fire, loving, and empowered. The remaining chapters in this book will explain, prove, and confirm this point; and outline these critical steps to wholeness.

Why is Wholeness so Important?

1. Jesus suffered and shed His blood for you to be whole. Living with fear, low self-esteem, insecurity, self-doubt, wrong self-definition, negative self-talk, loss of confidence, misplaced identity, wrong mindsets, and any form of bondage, grieves the heart of God. You are a child of the Most High God. Jesus paid dearly, and in full for you to live free. Living any other way is living beneath your inheritance. If you are a parent, how would you like to see your child suffer with emotional, social, and other limitations, particularly, when you have provided lavishly for them to live free and clear of all encumbrances? Jesus came to give us a rich and satisfying life. In John 10:10, He said: "I came that they may have *and* enjoy life, and have it in abundance, to the full, till it overflows." Living without wholeness denies Jesus the reward of His suffering.

2. Human beings are tripartite beings, with a spirit, soul, and body (1 Thessalonians 5:23). Wholeness resides in the soul. The soul space is the seat of the mind, will, and emotions. It houses the personality, memory, likes, dislikes, decision making ability, feelings, and all the distinguishing marks that make you a unique individual. Your soul has immeasurable worth and value. It is so valuable, and has so much worth that God did not, and will not replace it.

Your born again spirit is brand new (2 Corinthians 5:17). When you gave your life to Christ, God gave you a new spirit, that looks exactly like Christ (1 John 4:17b). Your body with its five senses or "earth suit" will be changed in heaven (1 Corinthians 15:53). You will have a new glorified body like the body Jesus had when He rose from the dead (John 20:19). The soul is the only part of you that will not be replaced. God has only one plan for the soul - renewal. (Romans 12:2). This is why wholeness is so important!

In Luke 16:19-31, Jesus told the story of the rich man and Lazarus. After death, the rich man clearly recognized Lazarus, remembered his own family on earth, recalled that he had five brothers, felt agonizing pain, and had the same consciousness and recollection in his soul, that he attempted to treat Lazarus as the beggarly servant he knew him to be on earth.

Like the rich man, every human being has a living soul that is eternal. It will live forever, in heaven or hell. So, you will remember what happened on earth, know your family members, friends and co-workers, recall the choices and decisions you made on earth, and so on. Jesus appraised the value of one soul higher than the value of the whole world. In Mark 8:36, He asked a poignant question, "What will it profit a man to gain the whole world and lose his soul?" Your eternal soul is of immeasurable worth and value.

This is why healing, restoration, and wholeness in the soul space is so important, because you will take your soul into eternity.

3. In God's relationship economy, 1 + 1 =1. No other combination gets to the same result. This is why it poses a major problem when a person who is not whole or complete in themselves, is trying to build a relationship with another person. This is a frustrating and painful enterprise because in God's relationship economy, ¼, ½, or 2/3 + 1 will never equal 1.

> *In God's relationship economy, 1 + 1 =1. No other combination gets to the same result.*

So many people desire to connect in meaningful relationships, but are not whole, and make no discernible effort to invest in the healing of the fragmentation and disarray in their soul space. They simply hope to meet the "right person" and make no investment in their personal growth and development to become the right person. Unfortunately, that is a prescription for failure. Investing in personal wholeness is the best way to prepare for future connections. Being whole will position you to attract whole people, bring a whole YOU to the table, and help you identify and stay away from un-whole connections. Wholeness is the best gift to give to yourself and your future relationships.

In math, whole numbers are numbers that represent unity without pieces. Whole numbers are positive numbers. They are exact numbers. There is no fraction or fragmentation. Whole numbers are unbroken numbers. They are integers. They are precise. This is why wholeness is important. A whole person is a positive person, a person who does not fall to pieces at the whiff of every wind of adversity, a whole person is a person who is clear about who they are, and can articulate with some precision what they want in life. A whole person is not fragmented, internally disjointed, and conflicted. They are consistent and when you deal with them, you don't have to worry about which person will show up today, because the same person will show up every time. Even before you get to know them well, you get the sense that they have depth and their personal foundation is sound, solid, and safe to build upon. They have the personal bandwidth and emotional range necessary to sustain a healthy connection and relationship.

Whole people are dependable, steadfast, and reliable. They have integrity and character. They are comfortable in their own skin, and take responsibility, and personal accountability for their lives, choices, and decisions. You don't have to do tricks or jump through hoops to keep a whole person happy. You don't have to exhaust yourself to fill them up by constantly pouring praise, affirmation, and recognition on them. They draw their confidence, self-definition, strength, and identity from their relationship with Christ. That supply never runs out, so they are refilled as needed, and have enough overflow to help others. A whole person always brings something of value to the table - themselves, and they always add value to any environment in which they engage.

When you've been with a whole person, you walk away feeling that you have gained from that interaction. This is why wholeness is so important. Wholeness gives life!

> *A whole person always brings something of value to the table - themselves.*

The path to wholeness is a process that restores the broken pieces of a person, resolves fragmentation in the mind, personality, values, thoughts, and beliefs; and provides integrity, consistency, and stability. Simply stated, wholeness allows you to know yourself, and confirm who you are, your values, what is important to you, your self-definition, and so on. This process of self-discovery, self-knowledge, and acceptance is critical to personal wellbeing, and is indispensable in relationship formation.

Un-Whole Connections

Un-whole connections are painful. They are connections between two people who are not whole or between a person who is whole, and another person who is not. Un-whole connections are fraught with difficulties, and here is why:

a. Trying to connect to a person who is not whole is a prickly and abrasive process because pieces of them are missing, dislocated or twisted up into a tangled mess. This could be emotionally, physically, mentally, socially, or relationally. They are not able to meaningfully engage and connect in the area that is lacking. Simply stated, things don't match up. It's like the lights are on, but nobody is home in the area of dysfunction. This can sometimes lead to the heartbreaking situation where you think you know a person, and then one day, a whole new side of them shows up, and you wonder, "Who is this person?"

b. Jesus tells us to love others as we love ourselves (Mark 12:30-31). Real love is built on a foundation of trust, understanding, and respect. How can you trust, understand, and respect yourself, when you don't even know yourself? Self-love that is not tempered by self-knowledge, and awareness is arrogant and narcissistic. And how can you love another person if you don't love yourself? When a person does not respect or love themselves, they have an insatiable appetite for love and respect that nobody else can fill. It doesn't matter how much their spouse or significant other pours into them, their self-definition is faulty, and because that core foundation is vandalized, the entire cargo of respect leaks out momentarily. It is an exhausting cycle of constantly trying to fill them up, make them feel worthy, respected, loved, and happy, and one single action, word or event undoes all that work, and you have to start all over again, because the leaky valve is inside them, and the solution must come from within. This type of laborious relationship eventually wears out the other person.

c. One of the decisions every person must make is who they are all by themselves. But, the person who is not whole, looks to others, their spouse, friends, and family to tell them who they are, and to make them feel loved, accepted, and valued. This places an unrealistic and undue expectation on the other person to be to them what only God can be. In time, they become demanding, whining, clingy, and a royal pain to be around. Their focus is entirely on themselves, as they are looking to earn, cajole, manipulate, or extort the approval, love, acceptance, and sense of value they so desperately need from the other person. Anything they do "for the other person" is really part of the whole scheme to earn or get them the compliments, approval, recognition, and affirmation they need. Eventually, this self-centeredness will pull the thread, and destroy the fabric of the relationship.

d. The person who is not whole will misinterpret and misunderstand words, gestures, and overtures. They have misplaced personal filters that color interpersonal interactions and everything that they see, hear or experience. They often read the wrong meaning into whatever is said and will interpret things in the worst possible light. Sometimes, they transpose the pain, distrust or trauma from a prior relationship into their current relationship, and exact from their current relationship, "payment" for past wrong, abuse or breakup. Sometimes they bring with them personal vows that they made to themselves - "Nobody will ever do that to me again." Sadly, because of these vows, they are quick to misdiagnose situations, and misinterpret words and actions. Relationships with an un-whole person tends to be stormy, on again and off again, like a roller coaster ride and often, they quit prematurely on a wrong assumption that most often is not true.

e. A person who is not whole, looks to another person to complete them, whether it is a child, spouse, friend, or other relative. They draw their sense of self-worth from being connected to or needed by this other person. This leads to a codependent relationship. Such is the cautionary tale of the person who gets married so that the other person can make them happy. This only leads to disappointment, bitterness, and disillusionment when inevitably, that person fails, as every human being does. Only Christ and a right relationship with him can fill the aching void in each of us, and our longing for meaning and significance.

Becoming Whole

Becoming whole is a process. It is a healing and restoration project undertaken, and superintended by the Holy Spirit. It is a multi-layered process that exposes and addresses multidimensional issues. Here are some steps in that process:

1. **Forgiveness:** The first step in the process of becoming whole is to forgive, let go, and release the person who hurt you.

    a. **First, Make a Decision to Forgive:** Most likely, you will not want to forgive or feel like forgiving. In fact, you may catch yourself fantasizing about some terrible things happening to the person who hurt you, as they "reap what they sowed" for all the pain they caused you. But you cannot let your feelings rule. You must submit your feelings to the authority of the word and will of God, and make a decision to forgive, regardless of how you feel.

    b. **Then, Begin to Say Those Words Out of Your Mouth:** Call the person by name, out aloud, and said, "I forgive you". It will be distasteful and heart wrenching.

You will not want to say those words. Even though you have decided to forgive, you still won't feel like forgiving. You may feel that the whole situation is unjust. The evil that they perpetrated against you was real, raw, and grossly unfair, and you may feel that forgiveness is somehow condoning or excusing those wrong actions. You may even feel cheated, used, and abused; but you must discipline yourself to follow through with your decision to forgive, and to say those words, again, and again. You will not believe them or feel them at first, but you must say them, out loud, over and over again as a personal commitment out of my mouth.

c. **Next, Go to God for Help:** Go to God in prayer, tell Him that you have decided to forgive, and ask Him to help you. Tell Him you simply can't do it on your own. God will ask you to surrender to Him, your right to hurt the offender back. You see, when you are hurt, you earn a right to hurt back the person who hurt you. This right is enshrined under the old covenant. Exodus 21:24-25 states, "an eye for an eye, a tooth for a tooth, a hand for a hand, a foot for a foot, a burn for a burn, a wound for a wound, a bruise for a bruise."

You have a choice. You can hold onto this "hurt right" and exercise it yourself, or you can turn it over to God, and set the offender free. That is the essence of forgiveness. Turning your "hurt right" over to God and leaving it up to Him to deal with it, and the offender as

He chooses. When you release the offender to God, you walk away free. Someone has said that when you forgive, the prisoner you set free is yourself. How true! Giving your "hurt right" to God does not mean that you forget or excuse what happened, or that you "reconcile", and get right back into the same bad situation, but it does mean that you will not hold, use, or exercise that right against that person any more. That right now belongs to the Lord.

d. If you choose to give your "hurt right" to the Lord, that choice will set you free. Forgiveness then becomes a gift that you give to yourself. It will set you free to be healed and whole. I believe that we are most like God, when we forgive those who hurt us. Jesus said that when we love, bless, and pray for those who hurt us, we are, sons of our Father in heaven, "For He makes His sun rise on the evil and on the good, and sends rain on the just and on the unjust" (Matthew 5:44).

Forgiveness and giving your "hurt right" to the Lord is the best way to make sure the devil does not win. The whole plan of the enemy in orchestrating the circumstances that hurt you was to destroy you, the offender, and all others involved. Forgiving the offender ensures that your life will not be destroyed, and relinquishing your "hurt right" to God, will ensure that, if at all possible, the offender's life will not be destroyed as well. God will work things out in such a way that the devil loses all around.

God owning, and exercising your "hurt right" is the only scenario that has the potential for a redemptive outcome for everyone involved. You see your real enemy is the devil, not the offender. They too, were deceived by him. If you take your eyes off the offender for a minute, and focus on the devil, who perpetrated all this evil, then forgiveness is the only path forward that spoils the devil and the kingdom of darkness. It denies the devil of the trophy of ruined lives that he worked so hard to get.

e. **Then Begin to Pray, Really Pray, for the Offender:** Pray that you forgive and release them. Pray for genuine repentance in their heart. Pray that it will be well with them and that God will bless them. Declare that the devil will not win in their life, but that God will win. Pray Ephesians 1:16-21; and 3:14-21 over them. When you start praying these prayers for them, you really will not want all these good things to happen for them, but as you pray, God will bless you and restore them. God will answer your prayer! Little by little, the pain, and animosity in your heart will decrease. God will peel it away, one layer at a time, like an onion. The things that you felt they stole from you, God will restore manifold. God will bless you so much that you won't mind or begrudge Him blessing them too.

> *We are most like God when we forgive those who hurt us.*

2. **Your Identity in Christ:** The next step to wholeness is to take back control of your identity in Christ. The devil uses trials to launch a massive offensive against our identity as children of God. In my book, *Choosing a Life of Victory,* I describe in detail the devil's multi step identity theft strategy.

The Devil's Identity Theft Strategy

A major challenge for men and women who have been or are going through severe trials, is how to overcome the devil's attack against their identity, authority, security, and sense of belonging as children of God. Here is the devil's multi-step identity theft strategy, not necessarily in any chronological order:

1. First, the enemy attacks your security and rest in Christ. He plays on your human need to understand and make sense of what happened. His favorite questions begin with why and where? "Why did you go through this and where is God when you need Him?"

2. Then, he challenges and questions your trust in God. How can you trust God? If He stood by and allowed these traumatic circumstances to invade your life, how can you trust him to protect you?

3. Next, he plagues your heart with fear! If God allowed that to happen to you, what else might He allow? He tells you, "you are on your own and anything can happen to you anytime."

4. Then, he attacks your faith and sows doubt and unbelief. When you pray, the enemy reminds you of how you prayed in the other situation and nothing happened. When you attempt to believe a bible verse, and stand on it in faith, he reminds you how you did the same thing before and it didn't work.

5. Next, he mocks your prayer life. What is the point of prayer anyway? Look how much you pray, and for what? Is your life any better than the lives of those who don't pray as much or at all? Look at your other relative who is not a Christian, her life is great, and she has none of your problems.

6. Then, he accuses you. You are a terrible sinner. There must be something you did to bring this upon yourself. If it isn't God's fault, then it must be yours. He then quotes the bible to you, sometimes through misguided Christians – you reap what you sow. So, you must have sowed this.

7. Next, he questions the faithfulness of God to His promises. God doesn't keep His word. Look at all the promises and prophetic words you received and believed in faith, all to no avail!

8. Then he derides your ability to hear from God and incites confusion. When you listen and believe that you are hearing the voice of God and want to respond in obedience, the devil shows up and asks you how you can be sure, really sure? After all, you thought you heard from God that other time too

and the outcome was bad. You were wrong then, how do you know that you are right this time?

9. Next, he challenges and tries to silence your witness and testimony. Look at your life, he snickers, it is a mess. How dare you speak to another person about God? What do you have to say? Your life is a reproach, who will listen to you anyway? Simply shut up!

10 Then he questions God's love for you. God doesn't love you. If He did, why are you going through this? God can deliver you, why doesn't He? Think about it, if it were your son or daughter, would you let him or her go through this if you can stop it? God doesn't care. He delights in seeing you suffer.

11 Next, he exploits the time element. This situation has lingered for so long and remained unchanged for days, months and years, despite your many prayers and faith. Why subject yourself to continued pressure, shame, embarrassment, and the crushing pain of repeated disappointment? It hurts too much to hope and believe again, only to be disappointed again and again. Just give up!

12 Finally, he goes for the foundation. He attacks the word of God. Since that scripture or promise of God that you have been standing on for so long did not come to pass, then the word of God is not true, the bible is a farce and none of this is for real.

This is a devastating cycle of attacks, and the devil is unrelenting in bombarding your mind with these thoughts. His strategy is extremely effective, particularly, if the situation has lingered for a long time. Over time, sustained pressure and repeat disappointment can pile up, wear down a Christian, and make him or her more vulnerable. The enemy's goal is to steal your identity and in so doing, your access to God's resources. He wants to render you powerless and impotent as a Christian, and ultimately, to drive you to hopelessness and despair. He wants you to be like the men and women that apostle Paul described in 2 Timothy 3:5, as "Having a form of godliness, but having no power". You see, the devil doesn't mind you going to church and serving diligently, as long as you live in defeat and there is no evidence in your life that you walk with Christ. This outcome achieves a two-fold objective for the kingdom of darkness. First, he can discredit God as a bad Father, and if someone else wants to become a Christian, he can point to you and ask them in disdain, "do you want to be like him or her?"

Pathway to Victory

Romans 8:31-39 outlines our response to the devil's attacks and gives us a pathway to victory. It tells us to talk back to the devil and gives us what to say. Even if you are still struggling to believe the word of God, do not understand what is going on, and cannot see or explain God's workings in your life, you can trust His heart and talk back to the devil with confidence:

1. God is for me – Tell the devil over and over again, God is for me. I don't know why I am going through this, but one thing I

know, God is for me. He is not against me. I am not in this by myself. God is for me (Romans 8:31).

2. God is not holding out on me. When I was still a sinner and an enemy of God, He gave me Jesus, the best that heaven had. If He gave me Jesus, why would He withhold anything - healing, finances, breakthrough, and so on, from me? God loves me, He will never hold out on me (Romans 8:32).

3. God chose me in Christ to be His child, devil, how dare you accuse me? God justified me and gave me right standing with Himself. I reject every voice of accusation and judgement (Romans 8:33).

4. No one can condemn me. Satan, I rebuke you! There is no condemnation for me, because I am in Christ Jesus (Romans 8:1). Every tongue that rises against me in judgement, I condemn (Isaiah 54:17b). Jesus is sitting at the right hand of God right now, speaking up for me (Romans 8:34).

5. Your best response to the devil's lies that God doesn't love you, because He allowed trouble in your life, is found in Romans 8:35-37. It states: "Can anything ever separate us from Christ's love? Does it mean He no longer loves us if we have trouble or calamity, or are persecuted, or hungry, or destitute, or in danger, or threatened with death? As the Scriptures say, "For your sake we are killed every day; we are being slaughtered like sheep." No, despite all these things, overwhelming victory is ours through Christ, who loved us."

6. I don't need to understand. Right now, I don't understand and can't explain what God is doing in my life, but I trust Him. I know that He is working on my behalf. Somehow, He will make all this work together for my good. (Romans 8:28).

7. Regardless, I will wait on the Lord. I will stay upon His word. I will serve, and I will worship. I believe the word of God that this situation is working for me. So, I fix my eyes, not on what I see, but on what is unseen, because what I see is temporal, meaning that it is subject to change, but what is unseen is eternal (2 Corinthians 4:18). Even if this situation on earth does not change, my eternal future is secure in Christ. I know the end of my story, and I win!

8. Declare Romans 8:38-39, proclaiming your victory in Christ! And I am convinced that nothing can ever separate me from God's love. Neither death nor life, neither angels nor demons, neither my fears for today nor my worries about tomorrow— not even the powers of hell can separate me from God's love. No power in the sky above or in the earth below— indeed, nothing in all creation will ever be able to separate me from the love of God that

3. **Accept God's Unconditional Love:** The next step to wholeness is to accept the unconditional love of God. The devil, other people and your own conscience will accuse you, but God's love will wrap around your heart, and hold you close. He will step up and speak up for you. His voice is like the sound of

many waters, and it will drown out the voice of your accusers. God will speak hot and holy words of tender, passionate love, and unconditional acceptance over you. Words like, "I love you", "You belong to me", "I will never leave you nor forsake you", "I know you by name, you are mine!" The Lord will cover and defend you. He will pick up every fragment of your broken heart and tenderly apply His healing balm to each piece.

4. **Immerse Yourself in The Word:** An indispensable requirement for wholeness is staying full of God, and His word. God, our Father, has provided all that we need to win in our battle against the flesh, sin, the devil, and the world. The arsenal is in the word of God. The word is both our offensive, and defensive weapon against the enemy. It is both our sword, and shield. The word of God produces faith (Romans 10:17), which gives us victory over the world (1 John 5:4). Very importantly, the word of God renews your mind, it changes the way you think, and sets you free from wrong mindsets, and strongholds. It helps you to exchange your thoughts for God's thoughts. It compels you to see things from God's vantage point, and gives you God's perspective. It transforms you, and helps you to identify and distinguish between the good, acceptable, and perfect will of God (Romans 12:1-2).

> *My feelings are not the truth. They may be the facts, but they are not the truth. The word of God is the truth!*

The Word of God is the mirror for your spirit. In James 1:23-25, the Bible says: "For if you listen to the word and don't obey, it is like glancing at your face in a mirror. You see yourself, walk away, and forget what you look like. But if you look carefully into the perfect law that sets you free, and if you do what it says and don't forget what you heard, then God will bless you for doing it."

This scripture makes clear that the word of God is the mirror that shows, and describes to me in detail what my spirit looks like. It tells me who I am, what I have, and how I look in the spirit. Things exist in the spiritual world that I cannot see or feel except through the word of God. But when I believe the word, I release those things, and bring them into physical manifestation. If I believe the information from the "word mirror" and act on it, (the Bible calls this faith), I will see change in the physical. How I feel is irrelevant. I just need to look in the spiritual mirror, believe what I see in it, and act on that information.

This is exactly what happens in the physical realm. The mirror shows me how I look physically, and I believe what I see in the mirror. If it tells me that my hair is out of order, and I take action to comb my hair in response to the mirror information, I will see the change. I don't "feel" that my hair is combed. I look at the mirror, believe what I see in the mirror and act accordingly.

Same thing in the spirit, it doesn't matter whether I feel sick, lonely, abandoned by God, or that my life is over. How I feel is irrelevant. I just need to look in the spiritual mirror - the word of God - believe what I see, and act on it. The word of God says that I am healed by the stripes of Jesus, (1 Peter 2:21-25); that I am a new creation in Christ, (2 Corinthians 5:17); that God will never leave me nor forsake me, (Hebrews 13:5), and that God has a great future planned for me, (Jeremiah 29:11). I must believe these truths, and act based on them. If I do, I release the power of God to change my circumstances. You see, my feelings are not the truth. They may be the facts, but they are not the truth. The word of God is the truth! When I believe what the word says, and act on it, I deploy the power, and grace of God to shut the door of sickness, loneliness, lack, and fear in my life. The truth of the word of God will always trump my feelings, and set me free to live the abundant life that Jesus died to give to me.

> *The state of your soul determines the course, direction, and outcomes of your life.*

5. Guard Your Soul: Wholeness resides in the soul. So, to be whole, you must guard your soul. Your soul is the conduit between your spirit, and your body. A healthy soul allows the abundance, lavish resources, and nature of God located in our spirits to come through the bridge of our souls, and be manifested in, and through our bodies. Therefore, the state, and wellbeing of the soul has a direct correlation to the state, and wellbeing of the body. In 3 John 2, apostle John makes this connection when he states, "Beloved, I pray that you may prosper in all things and be in health, just as your soul prospers."

This scripture is saying that a prosperous soul equals a prosperous life, and vice versa. This is why it is so critical to guard the soul. Proverbs 4:23 emphasizes this point even further. It states "Guard your heart above all else, for it determines the course of your life." Simply stated, the state of your soul determines the course, direction, and outcomes of your life.

As a Christian, my spirit is perfect, like Christ. But my soul is a work in progress. The word of God is the mirror that shows me what my spirit looks like, and in so doing, identifies the gap between my spirit and my soul. It shows me the difference between who I am in Christ, and who I am in practice. This gap analysis is very important to personal, and spiritual growth. It exposes me to my God-given potential, creates an awareness about my vulnerabilities, and produces a hunger in me to change to become all that God created me to be.

My soul is made up of my mind - my thinker; my emotions - my feeler; and my will - my chooser. My soul is in the process of being redeemed, and the level of victory I experience in life, depends on the extent to which I engage in the transformation process described in Romans 12:1-2.

1. **Mind:** The mind is the battlefield, and victory or defeat starts with our thoughts. Proverbs 23:7 states that "As a man thinks in his heart, so is he." Translation, the battle is won or lost between our ears. This is why God is very prescriptive about what we allow into our minds. The Bible tells us how to think, and what to think. First Corinthians 2:16 states that we have "the mind of Christ". Philippians 4: 8, instructs us to "Fix your thoughts on what is true, and honorable, and right, and pure, and lovely, and admirable. Think about things that are excellent and worthy of praise." And Colossians 3:2 tells us to "Think about the things of heaven, not the things of earth."

   How can we do this? How can we win the battle of the mind? Proverbs 4:23 tells us how. To guard our souls, we must take control of our thoughts. We must guard our minds from enemy intrusion and takeover. We must stand watch over the access points or gateways into our mind – our eye gate, ear gate, and mouth gate. Make no mistake, what you watch on TV, what music you listen to, what books, and other material you read, what you say out of your mouth and the people you allow to speak into your life, will impact the texture and contours of your thought life. And whatever is on your mind will eventually come out through your mouth and actions. This is why king David, the man after God's heart prayed in Psalm 141:3: "Set a guard, O LORD, over my mouth; Keep watch over the door of my lips." And Job had a similar commitment. In Job 31:1, he said: "I made a covenant with my eyes not to look with lust at a young woman." The message is simple. We cannot allow garbage into our minds and hope to live a life of victory. To be whole, we must take control of our thoughts, and to take control of our thoughts, we must beware what we allow to come in through our ear, eye, and mouth gates.

2. **Emotions**: In today's society, this is by far, the biggest danger zone in the soul. We live in a time and culture where emotions rule. They are fickle, fiery, and fleeting, but very powerful. For many people, their emotions are in the driver's seat of their lives. They are emphasized, exaggerated, and elevated to the status of truth. We have movies wholly dedicated to emotions, and emoticons have blossomed into a full-fledged industry. This extreme focus on emotions is aided and abetted by social media. People wear their

emotions on their sleeve, and share even the deepest details of their lives with thousands of "friends" from around the world who they do not know. Each post boasts a generous sprinkling of emoticons. Life is all about feelings, and to most people, that is all the reality they know. The popular thinking is that feelings are uncontrollable. And since you cannot control how you feel, conventional wisdom dictates that you can say, do, and act out exactly how, and what you feel. Doing anything different is viewed as being dishonest, lying to yourself or not being transparent. But that is not what the word of God teaches.

The Bible makes clear that we are not to be ruled, driven or controlled by our emotions, rather, we are to control them. God expects, and in fact, directs us not to live, act or react, based on how we feel, but to act, based on the word of God. Indeed, scripture teaches that spiritual maturity is a measure of our ability to rule over our emotions. In my book, *Choosing a Life of Victory*, I explain:

"A good indicator of whether or not you are a mature son or daughter is in your mind—how you think and what voice you follow. If you are ruled by your emotions, you are a child. If you cater to your flesh, you are a child. If you are led by your five senses, you are a child. If you know what is right to do but choose to act based on how you feel, you are a child".

3. **Will**: This is your decision maker. It is the part of you that makes a choice whether or not to act. Your will is the seat of determination, perseverance, resolve, fortitude, execution,

and follow through. Your thoughts drive your feelings, and your feelings place pressure on your will to act. This is the ultimate goal of the devil. It is the goal of advertisers too. They whip up your emotions, fill your mind with targeted information, and then bear down on your will, and drive you to take action based on that information. They yell, "This offer will not last long, pick up the phone and call now". Moving the will to act closes the sale and unfortunately, depending on the mover, and the action taken, can lead to a lifetime of sorrow, and destruction. Many a young man in jail today, some for life, were victims of emotionally driven action.

Connecting the dots between the mind, emotions, and will is critical, because it leads to character formation. Your thoughts produce emotions, your emotions activate, and move your will to make a choice, your choices form your habits, and your habits form your character, and ultimately, your destiny. This is why it is so important to take control of your thoughts, and stand guard over your eye, ear, and mouth gates.

6. Self-Definition:

A critical link in the chain of wholeness is defining who you are, and aligning your self-definition with your source. Knowing your source grounds you, gives you internal legitimacy, confident assurance, and personal authority. God is your source, so, you must be able to say to yourself and others with conviction, "I am from God". "He is my source of origin". "I am His image, and my self-definition come from Him alone". For a Christian, this firm conviction and affirmation is foundational to wholeness.

To be whole is to be restored to an unbroken, entire, undivided, full, and complete state. It is reconnecting with, and being comfortable with who you are at your core, and who God created you to be. It is seeing yourself through the eyes of your heavenly Father, and drawing your sense of self from Him. It is recognizing and embracing the reality that in Christ, you are enough!

Genesis 1:26 states that God created us in His own image. Because I am from God, I do not need to be defined, affirmed, validated or confirmed by people, and should not look to people for approval. My self-definition, validation, personal authority, and affirmation come from my source - God. His approval does not depend on my works, looks, performance, meeting social conventions, or people's expectations. People are fickle, but God is not. He is constant, and His approval is unwavering. If people's approval cannot define, validate or confirm me, then neither can their disapproval, rejection or ridicule invalidate or genuinely diminish me, unless I let it. It has only the weight I ascribe to it, and I can elect to deprive it of any weight and power to hurt or negatively impact me. Even if the individual's express goal and intent was to diminish or neutralize me, I can refuse to be diminished, and in so doing completely rob their actions of power. This freedom from people is so important to godly self-definition and wholeness.

Jesus modeled this for us. He "did not look to people for approval. In John 5:41, He said, "I do not receive honor from men." He did not try to convince people of His value or look to them to validate Him. He knew who He was! Jesus was free from people! Knowledge of who

He was freed Him from human opinions, good or bad, and released Him to be all that God wanted Him to be.

For a Christian, the path to wholeness is the path of freedom from the definition, approval, affirmation, and applause of people, and the world.

> *If people's approval cannot define, validate or confirm me, then neither can their disapproval or ridicule invalidate or genuinely diminish me, unless I let it.*

7. Personal Value: The ultimate goal of wholeness is to bring you to the place where you see yourself through the eyes of God. God has placed tremendous value in you—He calls you a son or daughter. Your value is intrinsic to your source, and so, is not dependent on external factors like your looks, peoples approval, your marital status, performance, who you know, what you drive, your net worth, and so on. Because God is your source, that source will never diminish in value. You belong to God and your personal value, authenticity, and authority flow from that relationship.

You are of inestimable value! If you ever question your personal value or doubt how God sees you, listen to what Max Lucado has to say:

> "There are many reasons God saved you, to bring glory to himself, to appease his justice, to demonstrate his sovereignty. But one of the sweetest reasons God saved you, is because He is fond of you. He likes having you around. He thinks you are the best thing to come down the

pike in quite a while. If God had a refrigerator, your picture will be on it. If He had a wallet, your photo will be in it. He sends you flowers every spring and a sunrise every morning. Whenever you want to talk, he'll listen. He can live anywhere in the universe and He chose your heart. Face it friend, He's crazy about you!"

To be whole, you must recognize and own your personal value. Whole people are men and women of tremendous worth who value themselves, own their personal value, and are confident in themselves and their God. Whole people value people, and treat all people with respect, because God values people.

Codependency - The Relationship Lie

Codependency has been referred to as the disease of the lost self. It is a dysfunctional relationship where one person supports or enables another person's wrongful behavior, such as addiction, immaturity, irresponsibility, and so forth. The most common theme of codependency is an excessive reliance on other people for approval and a sense of identity. A codependent person is someone who cannot function from his or her innate self, and who's thinking or behavior is organized around another person or a process or substance. In this context, people who are addicted to a substance like drugs, or a process, like gambling, or sex, can also be considered codependent. Codependency requires one person to be physically or psychologically addicted and the second person to be enabling or dependent on that behavior.

Common symptoms of codependency include:
   a. Intense and unstable interpersonal relationships
   b. Inability to tolerate being alone, accompanied by frantic efforts to avoid being alone.
   c. Chronic feelings of boredom and emptiness
   d. Subordinating one's own needs to those of the person with whom one is involved
   e. Overwhelming desire for acceptance and affection
   f. Low self-worth
   g. Over-controlling, manipulation and perfectionism
   h. Unhealthy clinginess where one person does not have self-sufficiency or personal autonomy

Breaking the Cycle of Codependency
Exposing the Lie

The premise of codependency - needing someone else to the point that you compromise, sacrifice, subsume yourself or lose your personal autonomy just to be with them - is a lie. The truth is that you can live a full, fulfilled, and successful adult life as an individual man or woman. God affirms every individual, as a person of tremendous worth and value, with a God-given purpose, future, and destiny. His plan is for every person to live a life filled with His presence, purpose, passion, and power.

Is Jesus Enough for You?

I cannot end this chapter on wholeness without asking you a question, a deeply personal question, "Is Jesus enough for you?"

This question is critical to wholeness because you will NEVER be whole until Jesus is enough for you. Unfortunately for many people, Jesus is not enough. Now, they don't say that verbally, but it is clear from their actions and preoccupation. For some, it is Jesus plus a child, for others it is Jesus plus a job, or Jesus plus a bigger house, or Jesus plus a husband or wife. What they don't realize is that nothing will be enough, until Jesus is enough.

When Jesus is enough, then you are released from the obsession to get whatever it is that you think will make you happy. Declaring that Jesus is enough helps you to shut down your "DIY" (Do It Yourself) operation. It keeps you from fenagling your way, "manufacturing" your miracle, or birthing an "Ishmael"; which simply means trying to "help God out", by attempting to achieve God's plans and purposes through works of the flesh and human effort (Genesis 16).

Is Jesus enough when His answer to your prayer is no? Is He enough when He says "wait"? Is Jesus enough for you in every season of your life? To be whole, you must decide to speak to your soul, and conclusively affirm that Jesus is enough for you; on the mountaintops, and the valleys, when you are lonely, feeling depressed or discouraged.

I am not talking about a stoic resignation to "your fate" or a resentful withdrawal. Nor am I talking about simply settling for the status quo. What I am talking about is a quiet resolve that nestles in the depths of your soul. A peace born out of trust in the goodness and fatherhood of God. It is a recognition that our God is Alpha and Omega, the beginning, and the end. He is the Lord of time and has your times in His hands. It is a willing submission to, not only His plan, but His process, and timing too. It is a surrender of your preferences, timelines, expectations, and dreams to Jehovah-nick-of-time and a calm, and sober trust that even if He delays by your timeline, He will never be late. He will be there in the nick of time. It is a settled contentment, and confident assurance in the plans, purposes, methods, and timing of God.

Your resolution should be, "Lord, I do not want anything or anyone in my life that you did not give to me". There is a practical reason for this. Anything you get without the Lord, you will eventually lose.

I think of my life as a home that God has built and furnished for Himself. Every piece of "furniture" is hand selected by Him and bears His imprimatur. Having anything in my life that I did not receive from the Lord will not match the décor of my life. It will be out of place, and out of synch with the overall theme of my life, which is Christ, and Christ alone.

In John 14:8-9, we read an amazing passage – Jesus was speaking to His disciples before His crucifixion. He said to them: "If you had known me, you would know my Father. From now on, you know him and have seen him!" Philip said to Him, "Lord, show us the Father, and we will be satisfied." Jesus replied, "Have I been with you all this time, Philip, and yet you still don't know who I am? Anyone who has seen me has seen the Father! So why are you asking me to show him to you?"

This is remarkable! Many of us today would think that if only we walked with Jesus while He was on earth, then we would be satisfied, we would be content, we would be happy. But here we have Philip, who walked with Jesus, in person, for almost three years, but he still wanted more! He said to Jesus, show us the Father, and then we will be satisfied. Another translation says, then that would be enough. You see, that is the lie of the devil. Nothing is ever enough. It's always one more thing, then we'll be happy. Well, Jesus told Philip what I am telling you today, if Jesus is not enough for you, nothing will be enough.

This scripture illustrates the point, that contentment is not about what you have or who you have in your life. It is a condition of your heart. Philip had the Father, but did not recognize what he already had. Like us, he was chasing the elusive "more". He thought it was still out there. He did not realize that he who has Jesus has the Father and everything else. Ephesians 1:3 states that we are blessed with every spiritual blessing in Christ, and John 14:23 tells us that if we love Christ and obey Him, the Father will make His home in us. Jesus is our access to all of heaven's resources.

Is Jesus enough for you? The sober reality is that you will never find purpose, fulfillment, and wholeness until Jesus is enough for you.

> *Nothing will be enough until Jesus is enough. You will never be whole until Jesus is enough for you.*

CHAPTER 2
WELL

There are many good words that begin with W. Words like wealthy, witty, wise, warm, wholesome, winner, and so on. But no other W word captures the essence of wholeness for a Christian like the word well. It is the critical first step to wholeness. This is first because "well" embodies and encompasses all the other words, and secondly, it is a powerful prefix. When placed before almost any other word, it can turn it into a positive and empowering word. Examples abound, including: well-made, well-spoken, well-behaved, well-adjusted, well-done; and so on. This is exactly what whole people do, they always add value to any environment in which they engage.

> *Whole Christians are well Christians*

During a night season of my life, I began a saying that has stayed with me and become part of my private lexicon. I decided, right in the middle of all the mess, that whenever anyone asked me how I was doing, I would simply respond, "It is well with my soul". This was my predetermined response regardless of how I felt or what was going on around me at the time. I determined that I was not going to complain, whine, bemoan my fate or speak about my present circumstance. Rather, I would make that simple declaration over my life. I took those words from Isaiah 3:10 that states: "Tell the godly, that all will be well for them", and the popular hymn by Horatio Spafford. Every day, in response to "How are you" inquiries from friends and co-workers, instead of saying "fine" or complaining, I would say, "It is well with my soul". In a typical day, I would make that declaration several times and it kept my spirit tenacious, and my mind focused on the promises of God, so that I was not overwhelmed by my circumstances. In fact, that saying became so much a part of me, that it has been associated with me throughout the ensuing years. So much so, that recently, more than a decade later, two people gave me Christmas gifts with the inscription, "It is well with my soul". That declaration of wellness was a healing balm to my soul and looking back, everything has turned out well for me and my children.

"Well" is a word that refers to every aspect of a person's being. As an adverb, it means good, satisfactory or thorough. As an adjective it means healthy, fit, fine, strong, thriving, vigorous, and free or recovered from illness. It also means sensible, prudent, advantageous, beneficial, profitable, desirable, and wise. Further, well is often used as an exclamation to express a range of emotions including surprise, anger, resignation, or relief. In other words, "well" can apply to or describe the state of our emotions, mind, will, and body. What a word!

> *How beautiful or handsome are you on the inside?*

"Well" is a key step and requirement for wholeness in the spirit, soul, and body. Our born again spirit is well, because it is the only part of us that is perfect. Since our spirit is well, complete, and settled in God, that perfect condition of our spirits can be carried over the bridge of our souls to manifest in our body or in the physical realm. This can happen in reference to a particular issue, situation or

35

circumstance, such that we are well in mind and soul about that specific situation. It can also be a generalized, more durable state of wellbeing, where there is an overall and enduring "wellness" in our mind, and soul. This prevailing state of established and ongoing "wellness" is where we want to get to. A place where we are not moved by what we see, hear or by our circumstances. Rather, our state of wellbeing is dependent on a transcendent perspective and understanding, grounded in the person, character, and purposes of God.

Wellness speaks of inner beauty, the beauty of a gentle and quiet spirit, a soul that is secure and at rest. A well person is always more beautiful or handsome on the inside than they are on the outside. That inner beauty comes from a close relationship with Christ, a clear understanding of who they are in Him, and their value in God's eyes. That exuberant confidence, strength, and poise radiates out from their well souls and permeates all their interactions.

First Peter 3:3-4 admonishes godly women:
> Don't be concerned about the outward beauty of fancy hairstyles, expensive jewelry, or beautiful clothes. You should clothe yourselves instead with the beauty that comes from within, the unfading beauty of a gentle and quiet spirit, which is so precious to God.

My question to you is, how beautiful of handsome are you on the inside?

There is no wholeness without wellness. As discussed earlier, wholeness resides in the soul, which is the seat of your mind, emotion and will. The soul space can be tumultuous. It is the arena of battle for control of our lives. Our born again spirit is perfect and indwelt by the Holy Spirit. Romans 8:16 confirms this truth. It states: "For His Spirit joins with our spirit to affirm that we are God's children". However, our bodies are earth bound, and before we were saved, was conditioned to living according to the dictates of this world. Our souls catered to our bodies and was conformed to the pattern of this world, until we gave our lives to Christ. Then the conflict erupted! Going forward, when our body wants to do things the way it is accustomed to doing them, the Holy Spirit intervenes and imparts the word and will of God about the situation to our soul. Our bodies rebel against what it considers an imposition or undue restraint by the Holy Spirit. It wants and likes business as usual, and resents the constraining or moderating influence of the Holy Spirit.

Now the soul is in a quandary. It is accustomed to acting based on the information it receives from the body and its five senses, but now there is a new sheriff in town. The new and strong urging from the Holy Spirit to do things differently, and deep inside, the soul knows that the Spirit's direction is right, but it is bullied by the body's whining, harassed by bombarding thoughts, and pressured by feelings which those thoughts unleash, to cave in to the demands of the body.

In Galatians 5:17, the Bible describes this raging warfare: "The sinful nature wants to do evil, which is just the opposite of what the Spirit wants. And the Spirit gives us desires that are the opposite of what the sinful nature desires. These two forces are constantly fighting each other, so you are not free to carry out your good intentions." Even apostle Paul was not immune to this. In Romans 7:18-19, he gives us a glimpse of this ongoing battle in his own life. He states: "And I know that nothing good lives in me, that is, in my sinful nature. I want to do what is right, but I can't. I want to do what is good, but I don't. I don't want to do what is wrong, but I do it anyway."

Given this ongoing battle in the soul, it is possible to walk in victory? The answer is a resounding yes, but it is not something that we can achieve in our own ability. It is the work of the Holy Spirit in our lives. Victory is sure when we yield to the Holy Spirit's leading. We see an example in the life of Christ. In the garden of Gethsemane, with the trauma of the cross looming large, His flesh and the devil mounted a major onslaught to keep Him from going to the cross. They pressured Him to exercise His human will to walk away from the cross. The Bible described the intense confrontation and agony in Luke 22:41-44:

> He walked away, about a stone's throw, and knelt down and prayed, "Father, if you are willing, please take this cup of suffering away from me. Yet I want your will to be done, not mine." Then an angel from heaven appeared and strengthened him. He prayed more fervently, and he was in such agony of spirit that his sweat fell to the ground like great drops of blood.

The battle was raging! Jesus could have caved in to His flesh and walked away from the cross. He could have saved Himself, but then He would have aborted the mission, because He cannot save Himself and us at the same time, so He chose us. After His intense agony and tears, He quieted His soul and brought it under the control of the Spirit. A quiet calm settled over Him, a deep resolve to do the Father's will. His emotions were no longer in charge, the Spirit was. He knew what He had to do, and He was ready. This transformation was so complete that when the crowd came with Judas to arrest Him, He was in such firm control of His emotions that He spoke calmly to Judas, instructed the disciples to show restraint, healed the ear of Malchus that was lopped off Peter, and calmly asked the high priest and his posse questions, all without any outward display of overt emotion. His mind was made up, His soul was subdued, and the Spirit ruled. At that time, it was well with Jesus's soul, not because God had removed the cross, but because He gave Him the fortitude to endure and overcome it.

What is a Well Soul?

A well soul is a soul at rest. A soul with undivided trust and confidence in God. A soul that is stable, solid, steadfast, and immovable. A well soul is a soul that is abandoned to God, has entrusted the ups and downs of the processes of life into the loving hands of Almighty God, and is content with the outcome, even when it is unpleasant, and does not match its expectations. A well soul is a soul that has tears in the eyes, but unflinching confidence in the heart. A well soul is a soul that is unperturbed by circumstances and that is fixed on God with an undivided heart. One word to describe a well soul is peace.

The Bible speaks a lot about peace. Lack of peace is a condition where a person is agitated, troubled, disturbed, fearful, or unsettled. Peace on the other hand is a quiet restfulness, a steady and unwavering resolve to confront challenging circumstances with faith, fortitude, and grace. Isaiah 9:6 calls Jesus the Prince of peace. And in John 14:27, Jesus said; "Peace I leave with you; my peace I now give and bequeath to you. Not as the world gives do I give to you. Do not let your hearts be troubled, neither let them be afraid." This scripture outlines the following truths:

1. **I Already Have and Possess Peace:** Jesus gave me His peace. So, I already possess the ability to have established and ongoing wellbeing in my soul. Right now, despite my circumstances, I have peace and it is well with my soul, because Jesus gave and bequeathed His peace to me.

2. **Jesus's Peace Vs the World's Peace:** Jesus makes a distinction between the peace that He gave to us and the peace of the world. So, the world does have peace, but its peace is unlike the peace that Jesus gives. The world's peace is dependent on circumstances and controlling our outcomes to meet our expectations. The world's peace makes human sense. But the peace of God passes all understanding, meaning that it does not make human sense. It is a peace like Jesus had when he was sleeping in the midst of the storm (Mark 4:39). It is the kind of peace that Peter had, when he was sleeping in jail, waiting to be

executed the next day (Acts 12:3-19). This is the peace that looks trouble in the eye with a steady, steadfast, and unflinching gaze of faith and trust in the name, character, and grace of Almighty God.

3. **I Am the Custodian of My Peace:** It is my responsibility to guard my peace, because I can keep it or lose it. The Amplified version makes this clear. It translates John 14:27 as follows: "Stop allowing yourselves to be agitated and disturbed; and do not permit yourselves to be fearful and intimidated and cowardly and unsettled". Simply stated, I am the custodian of my peace, and by implication, wellness in my soul. I can choose to not be agitated, troubled, perturbed, and so on, or I can choose to "allow or permit myself to be agitated, perturbed, and so forth.

These truths are the opposite of what most people think, and certainly very different from the lie that our society peddles; the lie that our feelings are free agents that have a mind of their own, and there is nothing we can do to restrain them. By contrast, the Bible makes us responsible and holds us accountable for allowing fear, agitation, and perturbation into our hearts. We are the gate keepers. We can choose our feelings and we can choose to act differently from how we feel.

WHOLE People Take Charge of Their Emotions

Wholeness requires that we take charge of our emotions. We have the ability and power to choose how we feel and how we act. We can choose to shut down negative feelings and substitute them with positive feelings. All it entails is maturity and growth in the soul. There is a misconception, that ruling over our emotions is being dishonest or inauthentic. But that is a lie. In the above example of Jesus in the garden of Gethsemane, He prayed passionately and wept desperately in His private time with the Father. But after that, He arose with a deep resolve and strength to face the cross. It does not mean that He felt no fear, or suddenly felt happy about His impending crucifixion. Not at all. His flesh still wanted Him to turn and run, but instead, He moved forward with intentionality and driven by purpose. He did not act based on how He felt. He took charge of His emotions, and acted in keeping with the word of God.

It is clear from His example that "well" does not mean perfect or a life free from challenges. Well people don't have it all together. In fact, it is the state of being well in adverse circumstances that distinguishes the peace of God from the peace of the world. This is what Jesus meant when He said, "I have told you all this so that you may have peace in me. Here on earth you will have many trials and sorrows. But be of good cheer, because I have overcome the world" (John 16:33). On the one hand Jesus says, "you will have many trials and sorrows", and on the other He says, "be of good cheer". This looks like a paradox or an oxymoron. The only way to reconcile these two apparent contradictions, is peace, His peace, and He modeled this for us in the garden of Gethsemane. It is Jesus' ability to look His would be murderers in the eye and calmly talk to one and heal the ear of another, that sets Him apart from the world.

"It is well with my soul" is a popular hymn written by Horatio Spafford and composed by Philip Blass. The hymn was written after traumatic events in Spafford's life. The first was the death of his only son at the age of two and the great Chicago fire of 1871, which ruined him financially. He had been a successful lawyer and had invested heavily in property along Lake Michigan's shoreline, an area extensively damaged by the fire. His business interests were further devastated by the economic downturn of 1873, at which time he planned to travel to Europe with his family. In a last minute change of plans, he sent his family ahead while he was delayed on business concerning zoning problems following the great Chicago fire. While crossing the Atlantic Ocean, the ship carrying his family collided with another vessel and all of Spafford's four daughters died. His wife Anna survived, and sent him the now famous telegram, "Saved alone...". Shortly afterwards, Spafford traveled to meet his grieving wife. When the ship passed near the spot where his daughters had died, the captain informed the grieving Spafford, who went to his cabin and wrote the words of this dear hymn. Looking at Spafford's circumstances, which paralleled that of Job in the Bible, "It is well with my soul" sounds like a cruel joke, but it was not. It is the truth that in the midst of life's tragedies, there is a peace, faith, and hope that transcends life's circumstances, that can only be found in Christ. This is why this hymn has endured the test of time and blessed countless generations.

Second Kings 4:8 tells the story of a "great woman", the woman of Shunem. She was a wealthy woman who took it upon herself to care for and support Elisha the prophet of God. So, she built an addition to her home to provide guest quarters for the prophet. She simply wanted to minister to him, but as always happens, God blessed her beyond her dreams. The man of God found out that she had no child, so he prophesied to her, "Next year at this time you will be holding a son in your arms!" "No, my lord!" she cried. "O man of God, don't deceive me and get my hopes up like that." But sure enough, the woman soon became pregnant, and at that time the following year she had a son, just as Elisha had said.

One day, while the boy was out with his father in the field, he had what appears to be a heat stroke. His father sent him home to his mother. He sat on her lap until noon and died. The Bible describes what happens next. "And she went up and laid him on the bed of the man of God, shut *the door* upon him, and went out. Then she called to her husband, and said, "Please send me one of the young men and one of the donkeys, that I may run to the man of God and come back." So he said, "Why are you going to him today? *It is* neither the New Moon nor the Sabbath." And she said, "*It is* well".

Think about that! Her only child had just died, a child that she had conceived against incredible odds. The Bible indicates that she had been childless for a while and her husband was old. The fact that she has lost all hope of having a child is evident in her response to Elisha when he told her that she would conceive. She said to him, "O man of God, don't deceive me and get my hopes up like that." So, having this child was a miracle and there was no real prospect of her having another child. Plus, the fact that the boy had died suddenly. There is no indication in the scripture that he had been sick. The Bible just states that:

> "He went out to help his father, who was working with the harvesters. Suddenly he cried out, "My head hurts! My head hurts!" His father said to one of the servants, "Carry him home to his mother." So the servant took him home, and his mother held him on her lap. But around noontime he died."

His death was sudden and traumatic. Most women would collapse and cry hysterically, but not this woman. Make no mistake. She was as distraught as any mother would be who lost her only child unexpectedly and in such tragic circumstances, but instead of falling apart, she reined in her emotions and sprang into action. She did not even tell her husband what had happened and when asked, she said, "It is well". This woman went looking for Elisha the man of God. When Elisha saw her, he knew something was horribly wrong. He sent Gehazi his servant to meet her. He said: "Please run now to meet her, and say to her, '*Is it* well with you? *Is it* well with your husband? *Is it* well with the child?'" And she answered, "*It is* well." This woman was unwavering in her confidence that God will intervene on her behalf and raise her son from death, and He did.

> *Make God your primary focus, and you will be at peace. Make the world your primary focus, and you will be in pieces.*

"It is well" is not a statement for wimps. It is not a wishy washy cliché. It is a statement rooted in a firm conviction that the God of heaven is a good God, and that He is who He says that He is, and will do exactly what He says that He will do. It is a statement that flows from a heart that is not ruled by emotions, but that is rested and nested in God. As I shared earlier, "It is well with my soul" was my personal battle cry during one of the toughest times of my life.

Ships are made for the ocean. It is their natural habitat. A ship's intended destiny is to sail the high seas. It is built specifically to perform successfully in the water. So, a ship is not threatened by water. For a ship, being in the water or surrounded by water is perfectly normal, and the ship is fine and dandy to be in the midst of all the water in the world, as long as it stays on top of the water. The ship gets into trouble when the water on the outside, gets into the ship. The ship can sail mighty oceans and be unscathed, but a relatively small amount of water inside the ship can completely destroy it.

It is the same thing with us as human beings and as Christians. Jesus said, "In the world you will have trouble". It's a promise, though not the kind that we would like to claim. So, having trouble in this world is not unusual. Jesus had a boat load of trouble himself. We are built strong, sturdy, and resilient to withstand life's storms. Like the ship, our maker prepared and equipped us to sail in life's turbulent seas without drowning or being overrun. But that is only as long as we don't allow the outside trouble to get into our souls. Like the ship, we get into trouble when we let the outside storm get inside our heads and heart. That is why the Bible tells us to watch over our souls with diligence. This is also why the devil aggressively targets our souls. We must be diligent, intentional and deliberate to plug any holes in our lives that would compromise our ability to stay afloat, and maintain a well soul in the midst of life's challenges.

How Can You Have a "Well" Soul?

1. **Keep Your Mind on Christ:** Isaiah 26:3 tells us that it is all about focus. Your focus determines your mindset and the condition of your soul. Make God your primary focus, and you will be at peace. Make the world your primary focus and you will be in pieces. How do you make God your primary focus? Fix your thoughts on Him. Think, speak, listen to, and meditate on His word. Isaiah 26:3 states that God will keep in perfect peace all who trust in Him, all whose thoughts are fixed on Him. Then it admonishes us to trust in the Lord always, because He is the eternal rock. In today's world where everything is slipping and sliding – values, morals, financial markets, and standards - keeping our eyes and thoughts on God will help us maintain a "well" soul, a soul that is not tossing and turning with every sound bite from the news media. A soul that knows that regardless of what is happening in the world, God is on His throne and His kingdom rules over all.

2. **Prayer:** The Bible states pointedly that prayer is an antidote to worry and anxiety, two major contraindicators of a well soul. Simply stated, prayer, with thanksgiving is a peace facilitator. Philippians 4:4-7 states:

"Don't worry about anything; instead, pray about everything. Tell God what you need, and thank him for all he has done. Then you will experience God's peace, which exceeds anything we can understand. His peace will guard your hearts and minds as you live in Christ Jesus."

Prayer is a peace facilitator.

This scripture establishes a cause and effect relationship between prayer, thanksgiving and peace, God's kind of peace. This means that if you will pray over your problem with a thankful heart, peace is the inevitable result. What is more, contrary to how most people think about peace, it tells us that God's kind of peace is not a feeling. It is a soldier, an armed guard on assignment, commissioned to mount guard over your soul and ensure that it is well, regardless of your circumstances. Peace would ward off intruders like the negative voices of the devil and other people; as well as intercept and neutralize interlopers like "what if" thoughts and thoughts of worry and anxiety. Also, peace would alert you to oncoming danger like negative traffic from the TV, people headed your way with an assignment from hell to frustrate and distract you, any incoming missiles from the devil, and fiery darts of discouragement, disappointment. and disillusionment.

3. **Renew Your Mind:** We have already learned that the battlefield is in the theatre of our minds and that we win or lose the battle in that arena. So, Romans 12:1-2 gives us a strategy focused on the mind and a road map to victory. It

tells us that the only way to win the battle is to renew our minds. What this means is that we exchange our thoughts and opinions for God's thoughts and opinions. Isaiah 55:8 states that God's thoughts are higher than our thoughts and His ways are higher than our ways. However, God has made His thoughts and ways available to us in the Bible. So how can we exchange our thoughts for God's thoughts? By learning God's thoughts from the Bible and applying what He says to our circumstances. The process is simple. Study the Bible, accept what it says as the infallible word of God and the final authority on all questions, issues and discussions, and then do what the Bible says. Romans 12:2 states that if we do this, our minds will be renewed or reprogramed with God's thoughts and perspectives. This renewal process will transform us, and equip us to know, and recognize what the will of God is, His good, acceptable and perfect will.

4. **Permit/Allow Peace to Rule as an Umpire**: God rules in our hearts and guides our affairs through His peace. This peace is His unique stamp that helps us to identify God's plan, confirm His approval, and decide between competing interests. Colossians 3:15, instructs every believer to "Let the peace that comes from Christ rule in your hearts". This scripture emphasizes that we have control over the state of our soul, and directs us to put peace in charge! We must let peace, the peace that comes from Christ, referee issues in our lives and call the balls and strikes, like an umpire. It makes the point that not all "peace" comes from Christ. There is a false "peace" that comes from conforming to the

world's system, going along to get along, being a people pleaser or from favorable circumstances. When we put the peace that comes from Christ in charge of our lives, allow it to take the lead in decision making, and establish God's rule in our hearts, we would have a well soul.

> *God's peace is a soldier, an armed guard on assignment, commissioned to mount guard over your soul and ensure that it is well, regardless of your circumstances.*

5. **Faith in the Character and Word of God:** Knowledge of and faith in the character of God is a strong soul stabilizer. It is the impenetrable trust born of an unshakable conviction that our heavenly Father sees us where we are and is deeply involved in all the details of our lives. It is a faith built on the solid foundation of the immutability of God's character, person, and word. God cannot change (Malachi 3:6); God cannot lie (Titus 1:2); God does not vacillate, and change His mind like human beings (Numbers 23:19). God can be safely trusted. He is all wise, Almighty, omnipotent, omniscient, omnipresent, good, and faithful.

The popular saying that "the devil is in the details" is not true for a Christian. For every son or daughter of God, our heavenly Father is involved in the details of our lives. Knowledge of that truth anchors our hearts in the midst of the storms of life. When life doesn't make sense, we can say, "Right now, I don't understand and can't explain what God is doing in my life, but I trust Him. I know that He is working on my behalf. Somehow, He will make all this work together for my good". Job modeled this truth so powerfully.

Even though he lost everything, his children, wealth and health, literally overnight, he said: "Though He slay me, yet will I trust Him" (Job 13:15).

This is the resolute assurance that in Christ, we win, no matter what happens! We may lose things, possessions, relationships, positions, or life itself. But when it's all said and done, we win. It is a confidence based on the understanding that the president is not in charge, congress is not in charge, the democrats are not in charge, the republicans are not in charge, and the devil is not in charge. God Almighty is in charge. Isaiah 33:22 articulates it clearly, "For the Lord is our judge, the Lord is our lawgiver, the Lord is our king; it is he who will care for us and save us". This scripture is a wakeup call for those who are trying to make the government their God and provider. Our God is Lord over the judicial, legislative, and executive arms of government, and only He can help us. Psalm 62:11 summarizes it in four words, "power belongs to God". This truth should minister peace to your heart. God is our King, we are plugged into His kingdom, we operate by kingdom principles and economics; and the laws of the kingdom of God governs our lives and affairs. This knowledge produces faith and freedom from fear, worry or anxiety about the future. It produces peace and wellness in the soul. We rejoice in the knowledge that Almighty God is on His throne and everything is going to be all right.

6. **Praise:** Praise and worship is a soul lubricant. It causes the soul to bask in the radiant sunshine of God's presence and to gaze into His glorious face. Praise is one of the most transcendent activities we can engage in. It elevates our vision and thinking above the challenges and problems that want to keep us earth bound, and enables us to soar without limitations. Praise unhitches our arms, legs, and neck from the burdens, yokes, and weights that hold us down and we can lift off to heights of unlimited ecstasy where we see our God as bigger than all our problems, bigger than all our fears, bigger than any mountain, any challenge, situation or circumstance. Praise assures our hearts that God is for us. It tells the devil that we believe God, no matter what. Praising God in the midst of adverse circumstances speaks volumes. It says, "I don't know why I am going through this, but one thing I know, God is for me. He is not against me. I am not in this by myself. God is for me (Romans 8:31)" Praise empowers you to see your situation through the eyes of God, and whatever direction you fix your gaze is the direction your life will head toward. It's like the hymn writer Helen Howarth Lemmel wrote:

> "Turn your eyes upon Jesus
> Look full in His wonderful face
> And the things of earth will grow strangely dim
> In the light of His glory and grace

7. **Break Curses and Demonic Covenants:** Renouncing, and breaking curses, and other demonic entanglements is a

critical piece in ensuring a well soul that is free from bondage and oppression. This is because most oppression is caused by demonic traffic and activity. Several times in the Bible, Jesus addressed sicknesses and other forms of bondage by casting out a demonic spirit, and once the demon leaves, so does the condition that it fostered, maintain, and supervised. There are demonic forces that are deployed by the devil to maintain specific dysfunctions in the life of a person or family. These are sometimes called familiar spirits, and the condition that they engender is called generational curses. Generational curses are impediments, disadvantages, or problems that run in a family from one generation to the next. They can manifest as a recurring failure, sin, character flaw, or calamity that befalls that family. They can also be strongholds of the mind, thought patterns, habits, and emotional bondage. An example of a generational curse placed on a person in the bible, is in 2 Samuel 3:29. As a Christian, you have the right and authority to terminate any curse, drown every voice speaking from your past and ancestry, shut down the operation of the wicked spirits supervising and enforcing the curse or dysfunction in your life, and deliver yourself to walk in glorious freedom in Christ.

The place to start is to renew your mind and believe what the word of God says. John 8:36 states that Jesus has set us free, and whom the Son sets free, is free indeed. The Bible also says that you are blessed and cannot be cursed and your blessing is irreversible! (Numbers 23:19). Galatians

3:13-14 says that Jesus redeemed us from the curse of the law and became a curse for us, so that we do not have to live under any curse, but rather, we inherit the blessings of Abraham. This means that, not only did God redeem us from the curse, He set up generation blessings for us. Abraham's blessings are ours. This is liberating truth, but it must be activated. When a person becomes a Christian, they are deputized by Jesus to exercise their authority, and break any curses operating in their lives and family.

When you gave your life to Christ. He forgave your sins, wiped your record clean and adopted you into his family. Colossians 2:14 states that Jesus, "Cancelled the record of the charges against us and took it away by nailing it to the cross. In this way, He disarmed the spiritual rulers and authorities. He shamed them publicly by his victory over them on the cross." So, no curse can stop God's plan for your life. Jesus paid in full for all that and broke the chains of the devil. Hallelujah! God has spoken good concerning you. Believe and declare it daily in Jesus name!

How to Break Curses & Demonic Covenants

1. Repent of any sin on your part that opened the door to the curse or demonic covenant to operate in your life.

2. Forgive anyone who sinned against you.

3. Declare that you belong to God, and are bought with the precious blood of Jesus.

4. Renounce every association with the occult. Repent of every way that you opened the door to demonic traffic in your life, and shut the door on the devil.

5. Cancel every negative word that anyone has spoken over you, and revoke every license you granted to the wrong people to speak into your life.

6. Destroy any tokens such as artifacts, images, carvings, souvenirs, gifts, or "family heirloom", received or connected with the curse or covenant.

7. Revoke every curse or demonic covenant operating in your life. Declare Galatians 3:13 - Jesus redeemed you from the curse by becoming a curse for you.

8. Bind the strongman familiar spirit, and the strongman spirit of bondage, and cast them out of your life (Matthew 12:29). Loose the Holy Spirit, the Spirit of liberty, adoption, and sonship.

9. Bind the wicked spirits sent by the devil to supervise and enforce the curse in your life. Terminate their assignment and shut down their operation. Then bind and cast them out of your life and affairs in Jesus name.

10. Declare your freedom and wholeness in Christ, because whom the Son sets free is free indeed. Proclaim

Galatians 5:1. Jesus set you free from every curse or satanic covenant. You refuse to be bound!

11. Declare that you belong to the lineage of Christ. The blood of Jesus runs through your veins. Silence any voice speaking against you from your past or ancestry, because Jesus has completely destroyed them.

12. Take communion, to declare your union with Christ and deliverance from the devil and his kingdom.

8. **The Spoken Word:** Speaking the word of God from your mouth will establish wellness in every area of your life. The Word of God is a bag of seed (Matthew 13:1-23). If there is any area of your life that is unwell, find the word of God that addresses that situation, and plant it in the soil of your heart. How do you plant the word? By speaking it forth in faith. The promises of God are voice activated. So, to have a well soul, cultivate the word of God in your life and launch it forth daily through the spoken word. "The Word of God coming out of my mouth, in faith, is the most potent weapon known to man. What this means, is that every word I speak is on assignment. Once I believe the Word in my heart and launch it forth via the spoken word, it will not return empty; it will achieve its creative purpose and assignment. It is unstoppable!"

> *The promises of God are voice activated.*

'Well" also describes physical wellbeing, but we will cover that in the next chapter.

Enemies of Wellness

1. Reproach, Shame and Stigma: These are the triple evil sisters of the devil. A reproach is an <u>expression</u> of disapproval, disappointment or disgrace. Shame is a painful <u>feeling</u> of humiliation or distress caused by the consciousness of wrong, indignity, and embarrassment. Stigma is a <u>mark</u> of disgrace associated with a particular circumstance, quality or person.

Can you see the progression?

i. First is an Expression of Reproach: This is something that someone says, shows, or does to you that expresses disapproval, disappointment or disgrace. This word or action becomes a seed planted by the enemy in your mind that begins the process of emotional trauma. Many times, the actual words spoken or actions taken were not even meant to be harmful, but the devil steps in and deconstructs or misinterprets those words or actions in your mind. Now, the words or actions become loaded with negative meaning or connotation for you and become very hurtful.

ii. Shame: You spend time turning those hurtful words over and over in your mind, until the negative connotation crystalizes, and is internalized. Now you see yourself through those words, and that misinformation, and reproach attaches to you personally, and produces shame. In your mind you see yourself as they described you and take on or adopt their negative description as an accurate assessment. This then leads to or compounds existing feelings and consciousness of insecurity, indignity, humiliation, and embarrassment, and you feel ashamed. By this time, what had started out as a comment about an action or situation, has become internalized as a reflection or assessment of your person. The most insidious part of this process is that the harmful effects of those words, depend only on the weight you give them. You can completely disarm and disempower them by denying them of any weight. For example, if you are an unmarried woman and someone calls you an old maid, that hurts only in proportion to the weight that you place on being married. If you don't put any weight on being married, their comments can roll off you like water off a duck's back. But if you place a lot of weight on being married, then their words can cut very deeply like a branding iron, and you think, "Something is wrong with me".

iii. **Stigma:** Reproach and shame if left to linger and simmer in your mind, will ultimately lead to a stigma, a mark, an invisible brand that you carry around with you, and something that scars your very soul. This mark or label mars you in your own mind, and places a limitation on what you can do, and who you can become.

The sad thing is that the expression of reproach that initiated this tragic cycle may be completely untrue. It could be a malicious, ignorant or mischievous comment that is not based in fact. But if you allow it to penetrate your psyche and linger, it could completely destroy your sense of wellbeing.

The book "Nothing" by Mick Inkpen, is a remarkable story of a little cloth tabby cat that had been forgotten under a pile of junk. It has been lying on the floor, in the attic, under heavy boxes full of junk, for many, many years. It has been there for so long that it could remember very little of anything. It had forgotten all about daylight. It had even forgotten its own name. I wonder who I am? He thought. It's owners decided to move to a bigger house to make room for a new baby. The movers arrived and the glare of a flash light stung its eyes. "What have we got here?" One mover asked? "Oh, it's nothing, let the new people get rid of it" said the other mover. The flash light was turned off and the door was shut. "Oh, that's my name", thought the little thing, "Nothing, my name is Nothing". The little cloth tabby cat began to call itself "Nothing". Soon, a mouse accosted him and said, "New people always get rid of you", "You can't stay here, not with new people coming." Then along came a fox who asked, "What on earth are you? "I'm Nothing" said the little cloth tabby cat. The fox sniffed at him. It's whiskers quivered. It's ears pricked. The fox said disdainfully, "Nothing worth eating, that's for sure", and trotted off. The little cloth tabby cat was devastated. It could not believe that it had been rejected, even by a fox. Finally, a live tabby cat named Toby came along and helped Nothing reunite with his family. He found out who he was. His name was not Nothing. His name was "Little Toby". He was a cloth tabby cat that was beloved and had a purpose. With a needle, thread, and some cloth, he was restored to who he was, Little Toby. And when the new baby was born, he was placed next to the baby.

Here again, we see the progression! The voice of the mover was the voice of reproach. He said, "Oh, it's nothing". The cloth tabby cat internalized those words, and began to call himself nothing. Then, everybody else began to call him nothing, and soon, they started to treat him as nothing!

I see this tragic cycle repeated in the lives of so many Christians. Due to wrong words, comments, and actions by friends, colleagues, family or church members, people are made to feel unworthy or on the fringes of society. Their self-esteem is compromised and they are emotionally vulnerable. The devil whispers to them, "Something is wrong with you". Then they go to school or work, and a classmate or colleague calls them "weird". At church on Sunday, they are given a cold shoulder by church members and made to feel out of place, invisible, and overlooked. Then they are not invited or decline invitations to go to church events due to insecurity. Now the devil is really talking to them. Everywhere they go, they feel fatally flawed or defective in some way.

Unfortunately, in many instances, this negative cycle is reinforced by family members who speak damaging words to this vulnerable person. They point at them and ask, "What is wrong with you?" This is a devastating onslaught, and sadly, this person soon begins to believe the lie. Next thing you know they are thinking, "Something is wrong with me". Then, most damaging of all, they begin to see, talk to, and about themselves as if something is wrong with them. Over time, this does incalculable damage to their self-image, self-definition, and self-esteem. They feel worthless, hopeless, and meaningless. And they begin to project that feeling or vibe of worthlessness to others. This sets them up for predators and manipulators, who would want to take advantage of them, and exploit their desperation and vulnerable emotional state.

Meanwhile, none of this is based in truth. None of these perceptions, comments or feelings are based in scripture. In fact, the Bible teaches that we must see ourselves through the lens of the word of God, and not the opinions of other people. And that you must say about yourself only what God says about you, not what you think or what other people say. This is the critical link – self talk. Self-talk is very important because it outlines the image of yourself that you have on the inside. Your self-image is crucial because what you believe and say about yourself has the greatest impact on your life more than any other person's words spoken over you. Your words can express negative self-talk, or it can reflect the tremendous worth and value that God has placed in you. Your words have the power of life and death. So, speak life over yourself.

2. Comparison and Competition: We live in a "social media" world. A fake world powered by cell phones, cameras and technology that can make the lives of others look flawless and exceptionally glamorous, and ours look humdrum by comparison. This set up can generate significant discontent, stress, and envy that erodes our peace, and undermines wellness in our souls. I once saw a program on TV where they showed a photo posted on social media. At first blush, it looked like the photo of a beautiful woman in a sexy bathing suit, lounging in a beach chair, with the ocean waves gently lapping at her feet, against the backdrop of majestic palm trees. She looked the perfect picture of glamor, luxury, and sophistication in a tropical paradise. Then they stepped back and offered a wide shot of the camera. I was shocked to see that the beautiful ocean paradise was nothing more than a paper backdrop and the lapping of the ocean waves against her feet was really the motion of water in a small tub. Her feet were soaking in a small foot spa! In reality, this woman was sitting in a beach chair in the back of a rather rundown house, but with the wonders of technology and social media, she was projecting a life of luxury that was completely bogus. What a stark contrast between what was projected and the harsh reality! When I watched that show, I wondered how many people had compared their real lives to the fake lives, and smiles presented on social media, and had envied that woman in the photo, and others like her for their "perfect life"?

Comparison is the act of considering the similarities or dissimilarities between two things or people. Comparison in and of itself is not bad, if it is a factual, sterile, outline and evaluation of reality. The problem is, that it rarely is. It is loaded with emotions, mis-interpretations, and personal judgements that are often woefully inaccurate. As in the story above, we rarely ever know the full reality of another person's life. We only know what we see projected publicly and comparing ourselves to them on that basis is flawed. "It's fairly easy to envy one aspect of another person's life – his/her figure, talent, wealth, significant other or intelligence. It's much harder to examine and then envy a whole life – a complete compendium of experiences". Nobody has a perfect life.

The Bible warns against comparing ourselves with others. Second Corinthians 10:12 states, "In measuring themselves against each other and comparing themselves with each other, they are not wise." Most comparison is unhealthy for the soul. This is because comparison has a twin sister named competition, and a partner in crime named envy. They blind us to the many things that God has blessed us with, and focus us on, and amplify, the few things that somebody else has, that we don't have. This is why President Theodore Roosevelt said that, "Comparison is the thief of joy". Comparison is corrosive. It eats away at our ability to be content, confident, and at peace.

Of course, not all comparison is bad. In 1 Corinthians 11:1, Paul said, "Imitate me as I imitate Christ". This is holy imitation. "Holy imitation is not about cramming ourselves into another's mold. It's about recognizing the Christlike principles another has applied to their life and figuring out how to apply them to ours." The key to holy imitation is, "Leading our comparisons in the right direction – away from envy, pride, covetousness, and self-pity, and toward Christlike imitation and the fear of God" (Dodds). This type of imitation or comparison can turn us into better parents, mentors and friends.

3. Strife and Contention: Strife is an unpleasant word, even its sound is unpleasant. It describes conflict, disagreement, argument, bickering, and controversy. Contention is the noise of relational strife. It is the quiet, seething, undercurrent of ongoing friction. Strife and contention are arch enemies of wellness, not only in the soul, but also in the body. Medical science has long linked strife and contention to a long string of ailments including, hypertension, heart disease, obesity, asthma, diabetes, headaches, gastrointestinal problems, and even Alzheimer's disease. This state of prolonged friction is very damaging to the soul – mind, emotions, relationships, and physical health. It breeds fear, worry, anxiety, and panic attacks. Strife and contention are the direct opposites of peace, are extremely hazardous to health, and are major contributors to an unwell soul and body.

4. Worry and Anxiety: This is when we focus on and meditate on our problem. Worry and anxiety is what results when we don't guard our eye, ear, and mouth gates. When we let the trouble around us get inside our souls, it breeds fear, worry, and anxiety. The Bible instructs us to fix our eyes on Jesus, who is the author and finisher of our faith (Hebrews 12:2). Second Corinthians 4:17-18 states, "For our present troubles are small and won't last very long. Yet they produce for us a glory that vastly outweighs them and will last forever! So, we don't look at the troubles we can see now, rather we fix our gaze on things that cannot be seen. For the things we see now will soon be gone, but the things we cannot see will last forever". This is the key to overcome worry and anxiety. Fixing our gaze on God and His awesome power and not on our problems. When we fixate on our problems, we look through the lens of fear, and "The lens of fear magnifies the size of uncertainty" (Chuck Swindoll). Also, worry and anxiety focuses on us and our ability to solve our problems. It fixates on our resources or lack thereof, and searches desperately within our personal resource pool for a means or avenue to meet the need at hand, and when we come up short, as we often do, it hits the panic button in our minds. However, God did not intend that we should live this way. In Matthew 6:25, He tells us not to worry, and in verse 27, He asks rhetorically "Can all your worries add a single moment to your life?" His point is the utter uselessness of worry. The only thing that worry produces are ulcers.

Sometimes, people are confused about the Bible's injunctions against focusing on the problem. They say, "I can't ignore reality". Well, the story of Abraham illustrates how we can elevate our focus and maintain our faith in the face of physical circumstances that contradict the promises of God.

In Genesis 12, God promised Abraham that He will make him a great nation. However, 25 years passed, Abraham got older, Sarah passed the age of childbearing, and they still were childless. Romans 4:19 says of Abraham: "And not being weak in faith, he did not consider his own body, already dead (since he was about a hundred years old), and the deadness of Sarah's womb". The key word here is *consider*. Another word for it, is meditate or focus on. Abraham did not focus on his daunting physical impediments. "He did not waver at the promise of God through unbelief, but was strengthened in faith, giving glory to God, and being fully convinced that what God had promised He was also able to perform." Abraham did not consider his dead body. He fixed his gaze on the immense omnipotence of Almighty God. Chuck Swindoll put it this way, "The size of a challenge should never be measured by what we have to offer. It will never be enough." Abraham knew this and so, instead of focusing on himself, he fixed his gaze on God. To counter worry, he gave glory to God, focused on the character of God, and verbally affirmed his faith that God will keep His promise, and God did. This is the pattern or model for us as well, to overcome worry and anxiety.

5. Guilt & Condemnation: These are the devil's favorite toys. They corrode our identity in Christ, attack our sense of value, and afflict our conscience. In the Bible, the devil is called, "the accuser of the brethren" (Revelation 12:10). He loves to accuse and heap guilt and condemnation on God's people, for what they may or may not have done. The goal of the devil in accusing us is to afflict, blame, and molest. He wants to undermine our confidence in our relationship with God. He wants to focus us on ourselves, our unworthiness, rather than on Christ's perfection, and complete atonement for us. His design is to create enmity between us and God and to alienate us from our rightful place and authority as children of God. He latches onto any issue, misrepresents facts, ascribes the most egregious wrong motives to our actions, and then impeaches our character. Unfortunately, because there is often some grain of truth in what the devil uses against us, we fall for the lie, and desperately try to defend ourselves or feel condemned, and unworthy to approach God or receive the good things that He has for us.

This is a strategic attack. Because a Christian robbed of his right standing before God in Christ, now stands in his own merit. That is a dangerous place to be. "When you step outside the new covenant in your thinking, then you are no longer relying on the victory of Christ, but facing off against the devil on your own merits. As soon as you take your eyes off Christ, you will see your sin and failure. Now the devil has you on his turf! He will accuse, condemn, oppress, torment and destroy you" (Godson).

Our pathway to victory is the cross and the finished works of Jesus Christ. Because of it, we can talk back to the devil. The Bible says that we overcome him by the blood of the Lamb and the word of our testimony (Revelation 12:11). We can talk back to the devil in the words of Romans 8:1. "Satan, I rebuke you! There is no condemnation for me, because I am in Christ Jesus (Romans 8:1).

Zechariah 3:1 gives us a vivid preincarnation illustration of the accuser in action:

> Then the angel showed me Jeshua the high priest standing before the angel of the LORD. The Accuser, Satan, was there at the angel's right hand, making accusations against Jeshua. And the LORD said to Satan, "I, the LORD, reject your accusations, Satan. Yes, the LORD, who has chosen Jerusalem, rebukes you. This man is like a burning stick that has been snatched from the fire." Jeshua's clothing was filthy as he stood there before the angel. So the angel said to the others standing there, "Take off his filthy clothes." And turning to Jeshua he said, "See, I have taken away your sins, and now I am giving you these fine new clothes." Then I said, "They should also place a clean turban on his head." So they put a clean priestly turban on his head and dressed him in new clothes while the angel of the LORD stood by. Then the angel of the LORD spoke very solemnly to Jeshua and said, "This is what the LORD of Heaven's Armies says: If you follow my ways and carefully serve me, then you will be given authority over my Temple and its courtyards. I will let you walk among these others standing here. "Listen to me, O Jeshua the high priest, and all you other priests. You are

symbols of things to come. Soon I am going to bring my servant, the Branch.

In this scripture, we see Jeshua, the high priest being accused by the devil. He was filthy, as we so often are, so the devil had the right to accuse and challenge him, but the Angel of the Lord (The pre-incarnate Christ), spoke up for Jeshua. He rebuked the devil, removed Jeshua's filthy garments and put a priestly garment on him, complete with the turban that declared, "Holiness unto the Lord". He silenced the devil's accusations.

This is exactly what Jesus did for us by His death and resurrection. Like Jeshua, we were guilty as charged, but Jesus took our sins upon Himself on the cross. He who knew no sin, became sin for us, that we might become the righteousness of God in Him (2 Corinthians 5: 21). Jesus canceled the record of the charges against us and took it away by nailing it to the cross. In this way, He disarmed the spiritual rulers and authorities. He shamed them publicly by His victory over them on the cross (Colossians 2:14).

Hallelujah to the lamb of God!

CHAPTER 3
HEALTHY

If you were asked to select an H word that accurately captures a key step to wholeness, which word would you choose? I looked at a word cloud for the letter H. Honesty and happy stood out above all the other words in the word cloud. This means that they were the H words most commonly used by people and would likely make the top ten of many people's favorite word list. Would you have selected them? What about words like holiness, halo, heavenly and humble. Surely, those words describe attributes and virtues that most Christians hold dear, and strive to model daily. Would you have chosen those words? Well, what about words like handsome, humor, hot, and hero. If you are a woman, you probably like those words because they are attributes that you'll want in your man! And if you are a guy, you certainly want those words to be used to describe you. So, would you select them? Well, more than thirty years of walking closely with Jesus has taught me that the one H word that articulates the next indispensable step to wholeness for a Christian is the mundane, hum drum, word, healthy! Healthy is indispensable to wholeness.

For starters, healthy encompasses many of those other H words, and for a Christian, it encompasses all those words. A healthy Christ follower is honest, holy, heavenly minded, and humble. Handsome, humor, hot, and hero is in the eye of the beholder, so every

Christian man can certainly look handsome; and every Christian man or woman can be hot, have a sense of humor, and be a hero to someone, even if only their kids. In fact, if he is truly living for Christ, I believe that any Christian man is undoubtedly more handsome on the inside, than he is on the outside. This is because God always works from the inside out, and He does his best work in the heart. Jesus in the heart produces a soul that is more good looking than any outward appearance.

Like "well", Healthy is a word that refers to every aspect of a person's being – spiritual, emotional, mental, environmental, social, and physical. The World Health Organization (WHO) defines Health as, "a state of complete physical, mental, and social wellbeing". More recently, WHO has added spiritual health to their definition. Man is a tripartite being with a spirit, soul, and body. To be whole, a person has to be healthy in all three dimensions. In other words, there is no wholeness without health - spiritual, emotional, mental, and physical. Health is a critical component of wholeness. This is why Jesus paid so dearly to purchase our healing. God wants us to be healthy in spirit, soul, and body.

Healthy Spirit

A healthy spirit is one that is indwelt by God's Holy Spirit. First Corinthians 6:17 states that, "The person who is joined to the Lord is one spirit with Him." So, spiritual health begins with a personal relationship with Jesus Christ. When we are joined to the Lord, His Holy Spirit comes to live in us; and the wholeness and perfection that is in God flows into our spirits and makes our spirits whole. The Bible makes this point vividly when it states in 1 John 4:17 that, "As

He (Jesus) is, so are we in this world". In our spirit, we look exactly like Christ because we are joined with Him. His Spirit joins with our spirit to affirm that we are God's children (Romans 8:16).

In today's world, many people claim to be spiritual and almost anything that involves any belief system can pass for "spiritual". But you need more than just any belief system to be spiritual. The belief system in question has to be able to answer the following four fundamental questions:

1. **Origin:** Where did we come from?
2. **Meaning:** Why are we here and what is the purpose of life?
3. **Morality:** How do we develop a moral framework, and make decisions about right or wrong, good or bad?
4. **Destiny:** Where are we headed and how should we live in light of that?

The Christian faith provides a coherent answer to these four questions, and therefore a framework for spiritual health.

Spiritual health is one of the four dimensions of health defined by the World Health Organization and has grown in significance in recent years. It has been described as, "The need for: meaning, purpose and fulfillment in life; hope, will to live; belief and faith". The spiritual dimension has been recognized as important for the overall attainment of health, wellbeing, and quality of life. So, "an individual with high levels of spiritual wellness will experience increased physical, social and emotional health"

Healthy Soul

A healthy soul is foundational to overall health. Third John 2 states, "Beloved, I pray that you may prosper in all things and be in health, just as your soul prospers." This scripture makes soul prosperity foundational. It shows that physical health and prosperity "in all things" flow from the wellspring of a healthy and prosperous soul.

"A healthy soul is at rest; it is not emotionally distraught. It doesn't worry or become anxious, fret, and fear. It is not burdened with guilt and shame. It has found its home in God and trusts Him to take care of all that concerns it" *(Joyce Meyer)*. The soul is made up of the mind, will and emotions. So, a healthy soul includes mental and emotional health as well as freedom from addictions and oppression.

Mental Health: The World Health Organization defines mental health as, "A state of wellbeing in which every individual realizes his or her own potential, can cope with the normal stresses of life, can work productively and fruitfully, and is able to make a contribution to her or his community".

Another definition of mental health developed by European psychiatrists is, "A dynamic state of internal equilibrium which enables individuals to use their abilities in harmony with universal values of society. Basic cognitive and social skills; ability to recognize, express and modulate one's own emotions, as well as empathize with others; flexibility and ability to cope with adverse life events and function in social roles; and harmonious relationship between body and mind, represent important components of mental health which contribute, in varying degrees to the state of internal equilibrium"

From these definitions, it is clear that mental health is a critical component of and can seriously affect daily life, relationships and physical health. Mental illness is a disorder that affects the mood, thinking, and behavior. It includes anxiety disorders, mood disorders, schizophrenia, psychotic disorders, dementia, and eating disorders. Sometimes, mental illness is caused by a chemical imbalance in the brain. Also, stress, family problems, and problems at work or school can precipitate mental illness or make it worse.

Emotional Health: "Emotional health is an important part of overall health. People who are emotionally healthy are in control of their thoughts, feelings, and behaviors. They are able to deal with life's challenges. They can keep problems in perspective and bounce back from setbacks. They feel good about themselves and have good relationships." Emotionally healthy people still feel stress and negative emotions like anger and sadness. But they know how to manage and effectively navigate these feelings.

Emotional health is not about the problems you have in your life, because everyone has problems. It's more about your approach to, and effectiveness in managing your problems. In her article, *7 Signs of Emotional Wellness*, psychologist and author, Dr. Shannon Kolakowski, outlines seven telltale indicators of emotional health. Below are excerpts from her excellent article:

1. **You Treat Others Well:** Emotionally healthy people treat others well. Viewing other people with compassion and treating them with kindness is a hallmark of your own well-being. Psychologists call this prosociality. It means that you tend to be sensitive to the needs and feelings of other people, and consider it important to help others. Simply stated, emotionally healthy people are others focused.

2. **You Like Who You Are:** Emotionally healthy people like themselves. When you are emotionally healthy, you generally feel pretty good about yourself. You know who you are – your foibles, quirks, and strengths, and you're okay with who you are. You're also congruent, meaning that the person you show to the outside world is reflective of who you are on the inside. While there are situations where you naturally shift your attitude or behavior a bit depending on the social circumstance, congruence means that your overall sense of who you are feels in line with what you show others.

3. **You Are Flexible and Adaptable:** Emotionally healthy people have the ability to adapt to all kinds of situations that life throws at them. When you are emotionally healthy, you are able to effectively assess your surroundings, your emotions, and other's reactions to a given situation and use these factors to decide the best course of action. You stand up for yourself when you need to, but you can also let others have the last word. You know how to have tough conversations, and set boundaries, but you also know how

to let things go. You approach life and relationships with openness, a sense of curiosity, and willingness to adapt strategy to circumstances.

4. **You Express Gratitude for Your Loved Ones:** Emotionally healthy people feel and show gratitude for the people and things in their lives. They purposefully look at life with a sense of appreciation for what they have, rather than focusing on what they don't have. Research has shown that counting your blessings has strong benefits for emotional wellbeing. Also, emotional health is enhanced by your ability and willingness to receive social support. This means that you have people in your life that you can depend on, friends and family who have your best interest at heart. Being emotionally healthy means that in your relationships, you feel safe to express how you feel, and you feel respected, and validated by those closest to you.

5. **You Are in Touch with Your Emotions:** Another sign of emotional health is that you embrace your emotions – sadness, anger, anxiety, joy, fear, excitement—as a natural and normal part of life. You know that its normal to have periods of stress, are able to manage and express yourself when you feel upset, and know who you can go to, to get comfort or help. You handle and acknowledge your difficult emotions without being overwhelmed by them, or denying that they exist. Emotional health comes from being able to identify, acknowledge, and accept tough emotions, but also move forward from them without getting stuck. Being

emotionally healthy means you might get nervous before going on a date, but you don't let that stop you from going on the date.

6. **You Have Meaning in Your Life:** Emotionally healthy people have a sense of meaning and purpose in life. Emotional health includes living beyond yourself and having passion, a mission, a cause, or larger meaning to your life. This happens when you use your resources to help something or someone that you believe in, for example, volunteering at your child's school, or at a religious or community service organization. Being part of something you connect with and care about is largely associated with emotional wellbeing and longevity.

7. **You Value Experience More Than Possessions:** Emotionally healthy people value people. "People who tend to highly value attaining wealth, popularity or attractiveness tend to be less emotionally well-off, than people who value self-fulfillment and helping others. People with high levels of emotional health tend to spend their money on experiences, rather than material possessions." Experiences contribute to emotional health because they lead to shared memories and bonding with people, help you enjoy the beauty in the world, and cultivate the positive emotions that come with new experiences.

Based on these signs of emotional health, how would you score yourself? On a scale of 1-10, what is your self-assessment? Are you emotionally healthy?

God Wants You to Have a Healthy Soul

As we learned earlier, the arena of the soul is the theatre of intense conflict and ongoing warfare. The devil targets and bombards the soul with a daily barrage. His goal is to destabilize, disrupt, and discombobulate. His favorite tools include fear, worry, anxiety, depression, suicidal thoughts, hopelessness, rejection, low self-esteem and low self-worth, guilt, condemnation, and so on. The devil mounts a constant attack against us in our minds and emotions, his ultimate goal being to bring pressure on our will to make the wrong choice, in thought, word or action. Wrong choices when repeated, develop a habit, and over time, habits build character and define our destiny.

While there is mental and emotional illness that is driven by chemical imbalance in the brain, many of the devil's nefarious activities and demonic oppression can manifest as mental illness. Several times in the Bible, Jesus identified and unmasked the devil at work, even though he was hidden under the cloak of sickness, infirmity, and mental illness. Again, and again, Jesus would identify the evil spirit at work, cast it out, and deliver the person. Examples include the mute man in Luke 11:14, the deaf and mute man in Mark 9:25, Mary Magdalene in Matthew 9:34, the woman with a spirit of infirmity in Luke 13:11, the demoniac in Matthew 8:28-34, and so on. These scriptures illustrate the point that deliverance is a very effective approach to dealing with the types of mental illness that is driven by demonic activity or traffic. Later in this chapter is a detailed, step-by- step, deliverance prayer outline to help you break free from demonic oppression.

How to Cultivate a Healthy Soul

Benjamin Franklin's axiom that, "An ounce of prevention is worth a pound of cure" is true in mental and emotional health as in other areas of health. The best approach to maintaining a healthy soul is to keep from getting sick in the first place, or to recover and bounce back as quickly as possible after ill health. As in other areas of health, exercise and diet are the critical building blocks of a successful preventative mental and emotional health regimen. Here are some steps for maintaining a healthy soul:

1. **Meditate on God and His Word:** Exercising your mind daily on the truth of the word of God provides required conditioning for a healthy soul. Joshua 1:8 gives us the prescription, "Study this Book of Instruction continually. Meditate on it day and night so you will be sure to obey everything written in it. Only then will you prosper and succeed in all you do." Meditation means to think deeply or focus one's mind for a period of time on something. It means to ponder, reflect, and contemplate. It means to turn over and over in the mind like the cow chews the cud. It also means to mutter or speak the words out repetitively. Meditation on the scripture saturates the mind with the thoughts of God and keeps the mind focused on God. Meditation is a soul stabilizer. It anchors the soul in God and leads to inner peace.

> *Take thoughts captive with words. Words can stop a train of thoughts dead in its tracks.*

2. **Stay in the Scriptures:** Regular study of the scriptures supplies the essential vitamins for soul health. Colossians 3:16 gives us the prescription, "Let the word of Christ dwell in you richly in all wisdom, teaching and admonishing one another in psalms and hymns and spiritual songs, singing with grace in your hearts to the Lord." The word of God is Jesus himself (John 1:1), so, if you fill yourself up with the word of God, there is no room in your mind for the devil to occupy. The word of God is Spirit and life (John 6:63). It will minister the life of God into every aspect of your being and drive away death, bondage, and oppression in all its forms. When you confront a stressful situation, whatever is inside you will spill out. If you are full of the word of God, you will respond to your situations with psalms, hymns, and spiritual songs, instead of bitterness, vitriol, anger, cursing and depression. This is the best medicine for mental health ever! First Samuel 16:14-23 provides a vivid illustration. It describes how Saul, the king of Israel, was tormented by an evil spirit, which manifested in depression, fear, anxiety, and paranoia, but whenever the tormenting spirit troubled Saul, "David would play the harp. Then Saul would feel better, and the tormenting spirit would go away." Singing psalms, hymns, and spiritual songs will give you a buoyant, healthy, soul free from bondage and oppression!

3. **Renew Your Mind:** Renewing your mind is the soul therapy prescribed in Romans 12:2. It simply means exchanging your thoughts for the thoughts of God. The word of God tells you who you are in Christ, what you have in

Him, and what you can do through Him (Philippians 4:13). Renewing your mind means that once you find out what the Bible says, you believe it as truth, and if your own thought on the issue is different or inconsistent with what the Bible says, you set aside your thoughts and replace it with what the Bible says. When you do this, the word of God will change you, guaranteed, because, God's thoughts and ways are infinitely higher than human thoughts and ways (Isaiah 55:8-9). So, when we receive God's thoughts, it elevates our thinking and perspective. God's word strengthens you, enables you to see yourself through the eyes of God, and empowers you to prevail over every devise of the devil.

4. **Take Control of Your Thoughts:** To have a healthy soul and win the battle of the mind, we must take control of our thoughts. "Who we are is shaped moment by moment by the thoughts we let into our mind and heart." Proverbs 23:7 states that "as a man thinks in his heart, so is he." In other words, we are the sum total of our thoughts. But how can we control the multitude of thoughts that run through our mind each day? Second Corinthians 10:5 states that we can capture our thoughts and teach them to obey Christ. Another translation says that we can take our thoughts captive. These scriptures make us responsible for our thoughts. This is wildly different from popular belief, that we are powerless to control our thoughts, and that they can fly in and out of our minds at will. As Martin Luther said, "You cannot keep birds from flying over your head but you can keep them from building a nest in your hair." Same thing applies to thoughts.

You may not be able to control what thoughts pop into your head, but you can control what thoughts occupy your mind. So, how do you take thoughts captive? With words. Words slice through and stop a train of thought dead in its tracks. It does not allow that thought to complete. So, if you have wrongful thoughts that pervade your mind, speak the word of God right in the middle of that thought process, and it will interrupt, arrest, and short circuit the thought. Then replace that thought with a different thought from the Bible. Philippians 4:8 gives us a list of thoughts that we can think. It says: "Fix your thoughts on what is true, and honorable, and right, and pure, and lovely, and admirable. Think about what it excellent and worthy of praise".

5. **Deliverance Prayer:** Deliverance from demonic oppression is critical to the condition of the soul. Jesus came to set us free. We must make a choice to live free. Galatians 5:1 declares: "So, Christ has truly set us free. Now make sure that you stay free, and don't get tied up again in bondage." This scripture is clear. We have the responsibility to maintain the freedom that Christ purchased for us. John 8:36 affirms our freedom in Christ, "So if the Son sets you free, you are truly free". Freedom is your birthright as a child of God, but you must guard and enforce that spiritual inheritance! So, if you are entangled in emotional bondage, oppression or substance abuse, you can be free! It's already done. God has done His part, the next move is yours. All you need to do is to appropriate the finished works of Christ, and enforce your deliverance. Prayer to break free from curses

and covenants is covered in chapter one, and breaking soul ties is covered in chapter 5. Below is a Deliverance prayer outline. Apply these steps to dispossess the devil, shut down his demonic operation, cut off demonic traffic from your home, and set yourself and others free from oppressive demonic influences.

How to Pray Deliverance Prayer

1. Declare that you are a child of God, an heir of God and a joint heir with Christ. You are seated in heavenly places in Christ Jesus. You are a partaker of God's divine nature and have the mind of Christ (Galatians 4:7, Ephesians 2:6).

2. Declare that you belong to God, and are bought with the precious blood of Jesus (Ephesians 1:7).

3. Declare that the Bible says in Isaiah 54:14, that you shall be far from oppression, and that it shall not come near you.

4. Declare that you are the righteousness of God in Christ. You do not stand in your own authority, ability or righteousness. You stand in the finished works of Christ alone (2 Corinthians 5:21).

5. Bind the strongman spirit of heaviness, and the strongman spirits of fear, bondage, and infirmity, and cast them out of your life (Matthew 12:29). Loose the

Holy Spirit, the comforter, garment of praise, oil of joy, and the Spirit of power, love, and a sound mind

6. Rebuke every spirit of oppression operating in your life. Speak directly to the spirit, for example, if you are dealing with depression, you can say, "You spirit of depression, I rebuke you in the name of Jesus. I shut down your demonic operation in my life. I terminate your access into my life and mind, and command you to pack up now and vacate my life in the name of Jesus."

7. Cut off every demonic traffic in your mind, life and home. Declare that God has delivered you from the dominion of darkness and transferred you into the kingdom of His dear son, who purchased your freedom and forgave your sins (Colossians 1:13).

8. Declare that you are an ambassador for Christ (2 Corinthians 5:20), and your home is the embassy of the kingdom of heaven. So, nothing defiled or unclean is allowed in your home.

9. Disallow access to every agent of the devil into your life. Declare: "Every person with an assignment from hell to distract, stop or limit me, I reject and remove from my life".

10. Declare, "I close every door that I opened to the devil through wrong thoughts and negative words. I refuse to walk in fear, anxiety, worry, doubt, and unbelief. In Jesus name, I declare that I am delivered from emotional trauma, depression, oppression, and addictions" Amen!

11. Take communion to declare your union with Christ and deliverance from the devil and his kingdom.

6. **Break Personal Vows:** Vows we make to ourselves can bring us into bondage. When a person has had a bad experience, been the victim of injustice, or has been mistreated, a natural response is to try to defend and protect oneself from going through that again. Sometimes we do this by making promises or vows to ourselves, like, "Nobody will ever treat me that way again" or "I will never be poor again". While this is understandable and sounds ok, it really is not. You are making a covenant with yourself that does not include God. It is a covenant energized by the flesh and relying on human ability. Also, it is a heart matter, and the motivation is flawed or questionable at best. Sometimes personal vows are vengeful. At other times, it is your attempt to take care of and protect yourself, and is really a vote of no confidence in God. You have to take care of yourself, because nobody, including God, is taking care of you. The focus of personal vows is yourself, your resources, ability, and oversight over your life. Personal vows can become blind spots that blind people to moral lapses, or can be used

to justify moral compromise, drive ungodly ambition, and lead people to sidestep their biblical convictions to keep the vows they made to themselves. A personal vow to "never be poor again" can drive an approach to wealth creation that overlooks biblical values. Also, personal vows can lead to a rebellious attitude to godly authority in our lives, and foster an ungodly independence from any "restraints" including the loving restraints of God and His word. Personal vows are the perfect setup for a "self-made" man/woman mindset. Simply stated, personal vows can provide a gateway to the devil to gain a foothold in your life.

How to Break Personal Vows

To break personal vows, take the following steps:

1. **Repent:** Talk to the Lord about the situation/experience or circumstance that drove the vow.

2. **Confess:** Confess the underlying lack of trust in God. Lay before Him every lingering resentment for allowing you to be mistreated, not answering your prayers for help, and so on. Tell God that you cannot take care of yourself. You don't even know what the next hour will bring. Tell him that you trust His working in your life.

3. **Forgive:** Forgive the other person who hurt, mistreated or abused you.

4. **Cancel Every Vow:** Renounce and revoke the personal vows. Since they were enacted verbally, you can undo and cancel them verbally. Jesus has set you free, and whom the Son sets free is free indeed. Declare that you walk in your freedom in Christ.

5. **Bind the Strongman:** Bind the strongman spirit of haughtiness, and the strongman spirits of jealousy, and fear, and cast them out of your life (Matthew 12:29). Loose the Holy Spirit, the humble and contrite spirit, the love of God, and the Spirit of power, love, and a sound mind

6. **Bind the Demons:** Bind the wicked spirits sent by the devil and his strongmen to supervise and enforce the personal vow in your life. Terminate their assignment, shut down their operation and cast them out.

7. **Plead the Blood:** Declare that the blood of Jesus purchased your salvation and deliverance, and that the blood is speaking over you, freedom, deliverance, victory, strength, favor and grace.

8. **Take communion:** Take communion to declare your union with Christ and deliverance from the devil and his kingdom.

Healthy Conscience

A key part of a healthy soul is having a healthy conscience. Our conscience represents the God consciousness in us. It is the inner voice or moral compass that helps us to navigate the questions of right and wrong, and make decisions and choices about what is good or bad. The English Oxford Dictionary defines the conscience as the, "moral sense of right and wrong, viewed as acting as a guide to one's behavior." The conscience has two components; 1) A built-in consciousness of the morality of one's own conduct, intentions or character; and, 2) A feeling of obligation to do right or be good. This is why people get a "guilty conscience" when they do not follow the dictates of their conscience, or have a clear conscience when they do. The Bible says that God has written His moral code in our minds and upon our hearts (Hebrews 10:16). This code is the conscience.

Steve Gallagher, in his article, *"The Searing of the Christian Conscience"*, draws a parallel with the physical body. He writes,

> "In the physical realm, the conscience is comparable to the human nervous system. When a person is wounded, he feels pain – the body's inherent means of alerting him that something is wrong. Likewise, when a person sins, the human soul has a warning system that sounds an alarm because the person's actions have wounded him spiritually. The soul-alarm trumpets, "Mayday! Mayday! Something is wrong! He senses that his actions are not only wrong but will also result in destructive consequences."

Since guilt, condemnation and other negative emotions can result from the state of our conscience, a healthy conscience is important to emotional health. The Bible speaks a lot about the conscience. First Timothy 1:19 instructs us to hold onto faith and a good conscience, and warns that rejecting either would lead to shipwreck. It gives us examples of people like Hymenaeus and Alexander who refused to listen to their consciences, and as a result destroyed their faith. In 1 Timothy 4:2, apostle Paul warns that through repeated sin and disobedience to the promptings of the Holy Spirit, our consciences could become seared as with a branding iron and insensitive.

Steve Gallagher, in his article describes four types of consciences.

Four Types of Consciences

1. **A Tender Conscience:** A person with a tender conscience is keenly aware of every infraction against the Lord. He recognizes sin for the ugly thing that it is and remains consistently open to the Holy Spirit's conviction. He is not looking to push the limits of sin to see how much you can get away with, but to avoid it altogether. Sin to him is a poison which must be eradicated at all cost (Psalms 139:24).

2. **A Wandering Conscience:** This is when bright and innocent faith is slowly supplanted by cynicism, the world's attractions regain their carnal luster, old idols are re-erected within the heart and once forsaken sins start to resurface. This is the process of inner moral decay that occurs when a

person allows sin to reestablish itself within their heart. If the person continues along this course, he will soon lose the sense of the evil nature of sin (1 Timothy 1:5-6, Titus 1:15).

3. **A Seared Conscience:** The person who willfully and habitually gives himself over to sin loses the ability to feel the spiritual pain of his sin. As his heart becomes increasingly calloused, the spiritual system God constructed within him slowly loses its ability to detect the damage being done to it. If the person remains in sin long enough, he can reach the point where he is no longer influenced by the Holy Spirit. He has become so hardened that he would not listen to and does not want to hear the Holy Spirit. If left unabated, this will eventually lead to the death of the conscience.

C. H Spurgeon described this process of hardening of the conscience. "It is a very terrible thing to let conscience begin to grow hard, for it soon chills into northern iron and steel. It is like the freezing of a pond. The first film of ice is scarcely perceptible; keep the water stirring and you will prevent the frost from hardening it; but once let it film over and remain quiet, the glaze thickens over the surface, and it thickens still, and at last it is so firm that a wagon might be drawn over the solid ice. So with conscience, it films over gradually, until at last, it becomes hard and unfeeling, and is not crushed even with ponderous loads of iniquity."

4. **A Renewed Conscience:** When a man in habitual sin genuinely repents, acknowledges his guilt and takes steps to

put it behind him, his hardened heart begins to soften, and he gradually begins to feel the conviction of the Holy Spirit once again. The Bible describes this process as God removing "the heart of stone" and replacing it with "a heart of flesh" (Ezekiel 36:26). Finally, this person is back in the place where God can reach him and help him overcome.

The human conscience truly is a gift from God, to help us to maintain a soft heart and an ear that is attuned to the voice of the Holy Spirit.

Healthy Body

God Made Your Body: The human body is an amazing and beautiful work of art made by our great and awesome God. It is also a very complex machine made up of many difference types of cells that together create a dizzying array of tissues and organ systems. These include the skeletal, cardiovascular, nervous, digestive, lymphatic, respiratory, reproductive, endocrine, urinary, muscular, and integumentary systems. These systems are populated by a multitude of organs that work synchronously, and in close coordination to seamlessly execute the highly complex daily operations of all human bodily functions.

Do you know that the human femur can support a weight thirty times that of the human body, making it even stronger than steel? Do you know that the human nervous system can relay electrochemical messages at a rate of 249 mph (400 km/hr)? Do you know that, "The human eye contains more than two million operational parts that process up to 35,000 bits of information every hour? It is one of the most complex organs in the body, second only to the brain."

The body is absolutely amazing! Which is why it is ludicrous for anyone to contend that the human body, with all these amazing feats and features developed randomly by accident. The level of precision required in the functions of the body, the mammoth organization that it entails for the systems of the body to complete all these functions in close coordination, and the fact that most of these functions are routinely repeated over and over each day, belies that claim. The Bible is clear, we were made by God. Psalm 139:13-15 proclaims this truth, "You made all the delicate, inner parts of my body and knit me together in my mother's womb. Thank you for making me so wonderfully complex! Your workmanship is marvelous – how well I know it."

Steward Your Body

Your body is the packaging that houses your spirit and soul. It also houses the five senses that enable you to connect with and function in the earth realm. You cannot fulfill God's plan for your life and for the earth without a body. Simply stated, we need our bodies or "earth suits" to function on this planet because only beings with or in a body have authority in the earth. Therefore, the state of your bodily wellbeing will determine your ability to execute God's plans and purposes for your life. Given the import of the body, it is little wonder how much time and attention the devil devotes to ensure that we neglect, abuse or destroy our bodies.

The health of your body is so important that Jesus paid dearly for it. Before Christ, every Passover lamb was simply killed for the sins of man. Jesus was the only "Passover Lamb" that was first scourged and then killed. Why is that? Isaiah 53:5 and 1 Peter 2:24 tells us why. By the horrendous stripes that tore His back to shreds, you and I were, and are healed. So, Jesus paid fully and specifically for your health on the cross, but God didn't stop there. Your health is so important that God made your body to heal and repair itself. With the right foods, drinks, rest, and other inputs, your body will heal and regenerate itself. And when an intruder comes in the form of sickness, it will dispatch its police force, the lymphatic system, to go to battle and intercept, stop, arrest, and eject the intruder.

God has done His part in taking care of our bodies. But as in most things, it is a partnership. We as caretakers or stewards of our bodies, have to do our part to ensure our bodily health and wellbeing.

Make moves, not excuses.

Physical Health and Fitness

It is hard to overemphasize the importance of physical health and fitness. An unhealthy body can severely hamper our ability to serve God and build His kingdom, or contribute meaningfully to society. Further, it could stop us from being able to fulfill our God-given assignments to love and care for our families. It is therefore of crucial importance that we invest in our physical health and well-being. There are individuals who have medical or other conditions that impose physical exercise limits. However, for many of us who are not medically or otherwise constrained, we need to take action daily to contribute to our physical fitness. As stated earlier, God has already done His part in providing for our health. Staying fit is our responsibility. It involves daily exercise and healthy eating habits. My challenge to you is to invest in your physical health. Make moves, not excuses. Here's how.

Five Components of Fitness: There are five components used to measure fitness in health clubs and fitness facilities. Tyler Read describes them in his article, *"Top 5 Health-Related Components of Fitness"*.

1. **Cardiovascular Endurance:** Also known as cardio-respiratory endurance, this measures the capacity at which blood and oxygen is delivered throughout the body to fuel continuous activity. The delivery of oxygen and nutrients begins all of our bodily processes, which makes cardiovascular endurance the most important of all the health and fitness components. A weak cardiovascular system can lead to multiple health problems, including heart attack and stroke. To improve cardiovascular endurance, you need to exercise at a sufficient level of intensity to elevate your heart rate. Your heart is a muscle and like all muscles, need exercise to get stronger. Cardio exercises like running, walking, biking, climbing the stairs, and so forth, can help improve cardiovascular endurance.

2. **Muscular Strength:** Muscular strength refers to the ability of your muscles to produce force. When your muscles contract, they produce force to overcome any opposing force. But as the opposing force increases, there comes a point where your muscular

contraction cannot produce enough force to overcome it. Increasing the amount of opposing force your muscles can overcome requires developing your muscular strength. You can do this through resistance training with free weights, elastic bands, body pump workouts, and exercise machines.

3. **Muscular Endurance:** Muscular endurance is a combination of both muscular strength and cardiovascular endurance. It is a measure of how long a muscle can overcome a force before it becomes fatigued. Whereas muscular strength refers to maximal strength, muscular endurance refers to how long the muscles can contract under a light load. To test your muscular endurance, pick up three pound weights and see how many times you can press them over your head before you cannot lift your arms up any longer. To improve your muscular endurance, you can engage in cardiovascular exercises such as walking up a flight of stairs, running, or riding a bike. You can also increase muscular endurance by eating a diet rich in grains. Grains are an excellent source of fuel associated with heightened muscular endurance.

4. **Flexibility:** Flexibility or the range of motion at your joints, is an important aspect of health and injury prevention. A few factors play a role in your flexibility, including how tight or relaxed your muscles are and the mechanics of your joints. Flexibility training comes in many different forms, with static stretching being the most common. To perform a static stretch, you need to extend the muscle to its most elongated state and hold it there for a time. Daily stretches help to maintain flexibility. Also, vitamins and minerals from natural sources support and maintain flexibility.

5. **Body Composition:** The majority of your body is made up of muscle tissue, fat, and bone. For healthy body composition, the most significant variable is your body fat percentage, or how much of your total body mass is composed of fat tissue. A high percentage of body fat is associated with multiple health problems, including bad cholesterol, high blood pressure, and diabetes. To improve your body composition, reduce your intake of sugar and fat. This combination has long been known to be the cause of surplus body fat.

Rest

A critical component of, and prerequisite for physical health and fitness is rest. Rest is the body's preventative medicine, and one of the most effective protections against sickness, injury, and disease. You think clearer, sleep better and feel more energized when you take time to rest. In today's world, being busy and overscheduled is the norm. "But living in a constant state of crazy-busy with overscheduled to-do lists have a profoundly negative effect on your health" (*Anderson*).

> *God cares more about your "WHO" than your "DO".*

Most people do not plan any downtime, rest, stillness, or relaxation into their schedules. However, our bodies were not created for endless activity and non-stop engagement. We need time to slow down, check out, unplug, and unwind. Medical science has demonstrated that adequate amounts of rest and sleep promote physical and emotional health, reduce the risk of accidents at home, work, or on the road, and support memory, brain activity, and effective decision making. God created our bodies to need rest, and He established a pattern of rest for us to emulate. He worked for six days and rested on the seventh day, not because He was tired, but to provide a model for us. He then mandated a sabbath rest as one of the ten commandments. Jesus replicated this model. Again, and again, He would take time off to rest and recharge (Mark 6:30- 31, Matthew 14:23, Luke 6:12).

I heard the story of a pastor who never went on vacation. He was always working and serving his congregation and community. Needless to say, he was burned out. The advisory board of his church pressed him to take time off and recuperate. But he was adamant. His response? "The devil works overtime, he never takes a day off, and neither will I". Well, during prayer, the Lord rebuked him and asked him why he was using the devil as his example?

God cares more about our "who" than our "do". This is why He wants us to rest. When you take time to rest, you acknowledge your dependence on God. Rest is your declaration that God is God and you are not. He runs the world and not you. Rest is your reckoning time to check in with yourself and ensure that you are aligned with the things and people that matter in your life. It is your humbling admission that you are a finite resource, in need of refurbishment and sustenance. Do yourself a favor and take a rest!

Body and Self-Image

As a Christian, you must not let the world cast you into its mold. Hollywood's definition of beauty is a size two woman. That is a lie. God made beautiful women in all shapes and sizes. I personally cannot understand how a grown woman can be a size zero. My immediate question is "Where are you?" I also wonder whether size zero is healthy overall and adequately supports the normal functions of a woman's body. The tragic tales of young women starving themselves and looking like a bag of bones to achieve this dubious standard is heart breaking. Not to mention the eating disorders and other dysfunction that it has engendered.

A Christian woman's focus should be on honoring God in and with her body. She must be a good steward of her body, not so that she can meet Hollywood's standard of beauty, but so that she can be a good caretaker of herself and maintain a healthy body, ready and fit for the master's use. So, as Christians the reason why we exercise and take care of our bodies is because it is the temple of the Holy Spirit, and failure to care for the body will give the devil an inroad to shorten or terminate our ability to serve God on this earth. However, as apostle Paul notes in 1 Timothy 4:8, compared to godliness, physical exercise profits only little. "For bodily exercise profits a little, but godliness is profitable for all things, having promise of the life that now is and of that which is to come." So, do not sacrifice godliness for physical fitness.

To be clear, I strongly encourage everyone to exercise regularly. I have a personal commitment to regular exercise myself. But as with everything in our walk with God, the motive is of utmost importance. I like to look good and I know that working out helps me to look good. But that is not the primary reason why I exercise. I exercise because it helps me stay fit, and take care of my body so I can be a better and more effective Christian, woman, mom, friend, sister, and minister of the gospel.

There are some people who will never be a size six, even if they starve themselves. So, the size is not the issue, being healthy is. Whatever is the healthy size for you, press on to get there and stay there. Be the best you that you can be. Compete only with yourself, to become a better version of you. Accept yourself and love yourself. Let that be your motivation. I work out at the YMCA. In the women's bathroom is a plaque that reads "I work out because I love my body – not because I hate it". That is the right attitude. Love your body enough to take care of it, after all, Jesus paid dearly for you to have a healthy body. Love God and His call on your life enough to take care of your body, so that you don't abort His plan for your life through untimely death or preventable disease. Love your children, family, and friends enough to take care of your body so you are not a burden to them or bring them sorrow, anxiety, and worry through your sickness. Make peace with your thighs and be confident in who you are! If you don't like what you see in the mirror, change it, because you can!

> *If you don't like what you see in the mirror, change it, because you can*

Same thing with the guys. Having a six pack is way overrated. Having a one pack, a heart of gold, and a life that honors God is way more important. If the truth be told, some images of body builders with bulging muscles and ribbed veins can be somewhat frightening. So, you don't have to look like a body builder. All you need is regular exercise to ensure that you run your life's race to the end and finish well. The Bible says of men like Abraham (Genesis 25:8); Moses (Deuteronomy 34:7); and David (1 Chronicles 29:28), that they died at "a good old age." God promises us long life. In Psalm 91:16 He says, "With long life will I satisfy you and show you my salvation." So, we have His promise of longevity, but whether we live long, how we live, and our quality of life depends a great deal on the choices we make to be good stewards of our bodies. I want to die at a good old age, healthy and strong. What about you?

Looking Good

God wants us to look good! He is a royal God. He created beauty and delights in it. He dresses the flowers daily with resplendent splendor and exotic fragrances. He wants His children to represent his grandeur. He wants us to look good. In Exodus, when He gave the specifications for the attire of the priests, He did not skimp or cut corners. It was regal, elegant, and incorporated a lot of gold, and precious jewels. In his home in heaven, the streets are paved with gold, and precious stones lavishly adorn his dwelling place. God is a great king, and He rules in pomp and opulence. He surely wants us, His children, to look good, however, we must look good within the confines of His holiness. God's holiness is an inward beauty, the precious work of the Holy Spirit within the heart. However, it manifests in the physical and is visible in how we dress, talk, what we do, where we go, the friends we keep, and so on. God's holiness calls us to modesty, in word, deed, and dress. This does not mean wearing no makeup, ankle length dresses, and so on. That is a misinterpretation of holiness. You can dress like that, but not because God's holiness requires it.

With the prolific use of social media and selfies, many Christian women have forgotten the biblical injunction to dress modestly. They flaunt their scantily clad bodies in selfies posted on Instagram,

Facebook and other social medial portals. For them the biblical phrase, "Lo and behold" has been wrongly interpreted to mean low cut tops that expose their body for all to behold. This type of behavior does not reflect the holiness of God. So, while it is true that ankle length dresses and head covering do not express God's holiness, it is equally true that wearing gaudy clothes that are immodest do not represent the holiness of God (1 Peter 3:3-4).

Healthy Attitude

A healthy attitude is one of the best gifts a person can give themselves. This truth is reflected in the popular saying that, "Your attitude determines your altitude". A healthy attitude is a positive approach to life that makes us more engaged, creative, motivated, energetic, resilient, and productive. It is a positive frame of mind, way of thinking, orientation, and outlook on life. "It's oriented towards finding the best solution(s) to any problems and optimizing your abilities, instead of doing the opposite. And it takes into account others' wellbeing".

A healthy attitude and thought process does not mean "playing ostrich", and ignoring the realistic facts of life, on the contrary, a person with a healthy attitude focuses on the facts, but incorporates hope and faith into their thinking about the facts. It means that you understand and acknowledge the facts, but are not overwhelmed, immobilized or paralyzed by them. Rather, you use that information as fuel to energize and help you explore solution options. A healthy attitude is a critical part of effective stress management, which in turn is very important to overall health.

Chuck Swindoll captured the colossal importance of attitude to overall wellbeing when he said, "The longer I live, the more I realize the impact of attitude on life. Attitude, to me, is more important than facts. It is more important than the past, than education, than money, than circumstances, than failures, than successes, than what other people think or say or do. It is more important that appearance, giftedness or skill. It will make or break a company…a church… a home. The remarkable thing is, we have a choice every day regarding the attitude we will embrace for that day. We cannot change our past… we cannot change the fact that people will act in a certain way. We cannot change the inevitable. The only thing we can do is to play on the one string we have, and that is our attitude. I am convinced that life is 10% what happens to me and 90% of how I react to it. And it is the same with you… we are in charge of our attitudes"

> *Your future is as bright as the promises of God.*

Dr. Alan Zimmerman agrees. In his blog, *How to Keep a Positive Attitude When You Don't Feel Like It,* he said, "There simply is no substitute for a positive attitude. It keeps you going when others quit. It releases an abundance of energy….an energy you don't even know you have…and gets you through the toughest times". The blog then quotes General Douglas MacArthur who at 76 years of age, said, "You are as young as your faith, as old as your doubt; as young as your confidence, as old as your fear; as young as your hope, as old as your despair. In the central place of every heart, there is a recording chamber; so long as it receives messages of beauty, hope, cheer and courage; so long as you are young. When the wires are all down and your heart is covered with snows of pessimism and the ice of cynicism, then and only then are you grown old".

A healthy attitude will keep you young, vibrant, hopeful, and full of life, regardless of your age, circumstances, social or economic status. A healthy attitude is foundational to overall health.

How to Develop A Healthy Attitude

1. **Have Faith in God:** Faith is placing complete trust and confidence in someone or something. Placing your faith in God is the most stable, sure and enduring foundation for a healthy attitude. It is believing in the best future that God has for you. God loves you. He created you and has a great plan for your life (Jeremiah 29:11). God believes in you and He empowers you to believe in yourself. He is good and has the blueprint for your future. So, having faith in God and His precious promises will keep your outlook positive, and your future as bright as the promises of God.

> *Choose your thoughts carefully, because when you choose your thoughts, you choose your attitude.*

2. **Guard Your Mind:** Your mind has a lot to do with your attitude. If you have a sour, negative, and grumpy attitude, it is more than likely that you have been thinking sour, negative, and grumpy thoughts. So, choose your thoughts carefully, because when you choose your thoughts, you choose your attitude. This is why the Bible tells us what

thoughts to populate our minds with. To have a healthy attitude, fill your mind with thoughts that are true, noble, right, pure, lovely, and honorable (Philippians 4:8).

3. **Be Grateful:** Gratitude is a personal decision to call to mind the good people and things that grace and bless your life; and to take action to recognize and express your appreciation to and for them. It is an act of the will, so you can choose to be and act grateful, even when you don't feel grateful. Being grateful is to remember, memorialize, and treasure the people, things and relationships that give our lives meaning. Gratitude can bring a smile to your face, laughter to your lips, or a tear to your eye, but the posture of the heart is the same – simply and deeply thankful. Often during or at the end of a particularly grueling day, when I am tired and tempted to be downcast, I say to God, under my breath, over, and over again, "I am tired but thankful." This helps me stay focused on the positive and maintain a good attitude. Gratitude enriches your life, as well as the lives of others, and gives you a fresh wind for the next sail. A healthy attitude is an attitude of gratitude, and an attitude of gratitude leads to wholeness. Luke 17:11-19 tells the story of ten men whom Jesus healed of leprosy, but only one of them came back to say, "Thank you". Jesus said to him, "Your faith has made you whole". The other nine lepers were healed, but only this man was healed and made whole. Parts of his body that had been ravaged by leprosy were replaced and restored to wholeness because he showed gratitude.

4. **Do the Next Thing**: Having a healthy daily routine is a great boost to a healthy attitude. It provides the personal discipline that helps you to keep going and not wallow in the ditch of self-pity or despair when life hits you hard. A healthy daily routine gives structure to your life and enables you to make good decisions when you are emotionally vulnerable. This is because the good decisions were already premade and loaded into your daily or weekly routine. So, all you need to do to get through a tough day, with a good attitude, is to "Do the next thing".

5. **Don't Set Unrealistic Goals:** There are few things as damaging to a healthy attitude as setting unrealistic goals. It leads to disappointment, disillusionment, and discouragement. Goal setting is great, but setting unrealistic goals or expectations is a set up for a big crash, followed by resentment, self-pity, and a host of other negative emotions and attitudes. To cultivate and maintain a healthy attitude, set realistic goals.

> *God believes in you and He empowers you to believe in yourself.*

6. **Self-Talk:** Self-talk is the endless stream of unspoken thoughts that run through your head. If these thoughts are mostly negative, then your outlook on life is likely to be pessimistic, and vice versa. "Winners say *I can*. That confidence comes from a deeper I AM. For a believer, that confidence comes from knowing who I am and whose I am. I belong to God. I am a son or daughter of Almighty God. I am seated in heavenly places in Christ Jesus. All things are

possible to me because I believe. I *am* so I *can*. Philippians 4:13 (AMP) states, "I can do all things through Him who strengthens *and* empowers me. I am self-sufficient in Christ's sufficiency; I am ready for anything and equal to anything through Him who infuses me with inner strength and confident peace." This verse is the winners creed, and it begins with I *can*. Conversely, losers say: *I don't think I can*. That lack of confidence, hesitation, and self-doubt comes from a deeper *I don't think I am*" (Godson). Positive self-talk promotes a healthy attitude.

7. **Celebrate Yourself and Others:** Taking the time to celebrate yourself and others cultivates and supports a healthy attitude. To celebrate yourself is to rejoice and be thankful for your accomplishments, even the "little" ones. You don't have to wait for the grand finale to celebrate. You can have "bitesize" celebrations along the way. When I am doing a big project or have a busy day with a long list of to dos, one of the ways, I keep a good attitude is to stop in the middle of the work, survey what we have already accomplished and say aloud to myself and whoever is working with me, "Little by little, we are getting done!" This declaration tends to boost our energy and keep us motivated. My daughter looks forward to these little celebrations. When we are working together and I pause, look up and smile, she knows what is coming, and she joins me in the joyful celebration of our interim, incremental accomplishments. Together we say with gusto, "Little by little, we are getting done!" This is exactly what God did

when He created the world. Genesis 1 gives us the account of creation. It states that God would periodically pause, survey everything that He has already created and say aloud that, "It was good". I encourage you to do the same thing. Celebrate your "little" accomplishments. The Bible tells us to rejoice with those who rejoice. A great way to do that, is to celebrate them and their incremental accomplishments, whether it is a child, spouse, co-worker or friend, this would greatly encourage them to stay the course and finish well.

8. **Make Your Own Sunshine:** If you do, you'll never have another "rainy day". How do you make your own sunshine? By counting your blessings and remembering that you have so much to be thankful for. One of my most frequent prayers under my breath is, "Thank you Lord". On days when I am sensing the beginnings of sadness, or when something happens that threatens to warp my focus and narrow my vision to the few things in life that I don't have, I remember and begin to verbally thank God, under my breath for seemingly little things, like the fact that I woke up this morning, with a good head on my shoulders. I thank Him for indoor plumbing, a hot shower, for the food on my table, money in my pocket, the blessing of family and friends, the fact that I can drive, that my eyes can see the beautiful world He created, and so on. Every time I go to the store, I leave with a grateful heart, thanking the Lord that I am able to purchase what we need without worrying about how to pay for it. I rejoice in His lavish provision for all our needs. Without fail, my spirit is lifted and I think, "God sees me right

now, He knows exactly where I am, I may not have a plan, but He does." Apostle Paul was a super model of this principle. While in jail, he wrote the letter to the Philippians. These are some of the most uplifting and joyful verses in the entire Bible. He booms, "Rejoice in the Lord always, and again I say rejoice!" Unbelievable! This is a guy incarcerated in an underground dungeon, probably with open sewer running close by. But that did not stop him because he makes his own sunshine. You can too!

9. **Take Personal Responsibility for Your Life:** Taking personal responsibility for your life is empowering and is indispensable to a healthy attitude. Your motto should be, "See it, own it, solve it, and do it". This takes away your excuses. It says to you, "It may not be your fault, but it is your responsibility and you can fix it". It activates the I CAN" in you. Conversely, whenever you blame someone else, you abdicate responsibility for your life and become powerless to change your situation. If it is somebody else's fault, then you are powerless to fix it. But when you take personal responsibility, you reclaim your power and are able to bring about needed change. A healthy attitude which takes personal responsibility puts you in charge and empowers you to win.

> *Make your own sunshine and you'll never have another "rainy day!"*

10. **Value People:** A fundamental requirement to a healthy attitude is valuing people, including yourself. It is recognizing that you are a person of tremendous worth and value, and

identifying, growing, and owning your personal value. Valuing people promotes a healthy attitude, because it helps to balance your perspective, makes you resilient, and enables you to believe in yourself to overcome life's obstacles.

11. **See Failure and Setback as an Opportunity:** Failure, setback and hardship are some of the best teachers in the world. They keep us humble, empathetic, and teachable. A healthy attitude sees failure as an opportunity to grow, learn, become better, and excel. So many times in my life, a situation that I thought was the worst thing to ever happen, eventually turns out to be a blessing in disguise. The Poem, *"Along the Road"* by Robert Browning Hamilton's captures the essence of the value of failure and setback in our lives. He writes:

I walked a mile with Pleasure
She chatted all the way,
But left me none the wiser
For all she had to say.

I walked a mile with Sorrow
And ne're a word said she;
But oh, the things I learned from her
When Sorrow walked with me!

CHAPTER 4
ON-FIRE

An indispensable step to wholeness is a passionate love for Jesus. Whole Christians are ablaze with a passionate, committed love for Jesus and a burning desire to help people. First Corinthians 7:34 states that we should "Be devoted to the Lord and holy in body and in spirit". Simply stated, we can and should be on-fire for God! We should have hearts, passions, and appetites that are singularly focused, red-hot, tuned in, and fully devoted to God. Christians should never feel uncommitted. We should always feel committed in our relationship to Jesus Christ.

The dictionary defines "on-fire" as, ablaze, fiery, ardent, passionate, fervent, intense and excited. The Urban Dictionary defines it as, "A term that people use when someone is doing great and they are unable to be stopped." In other words, to be "on fire" is to be fully energized, actively engaged, keenly aware, unstoppable, and living life on full throttle with all cylinders firing. What a sharp contrast to the way many Christians live today – merely existing, disengaged, listless, with no joy, excitement, expectancy or fervency. Many have checked out on life and are merely going through the motions, simply surviving. Others are coasting through life on auto pilot.

However, passion, zeal, and zest for life is a critical component of wholeness. To be whole, a person has to be on-fire in all three dimensions. In other words, there is no wholeness without passion, and zest - spiritually, emotionally, and physically. It is this zeal, expectancy, and thrust that gets you out of bed each morning with a bounce. It is this confluence of passion, zeal, and fire that fuels purpose, drives productivity, and a positive outlook on life.

Where Did the Fire Go?

The lives of many Christians are marked by apathy and indifference. Some of the indifference is fueled by repeated disappointment and disillusionment. Many have endured prolonged hoping, praying, and believing for a healing, financial breakthrough, salvation of a family member, family restoration, or some other situation to change, only to be disappointed, again and again. Over time, the pain of repeated disappointment becomes too much to bear, so they stop believing, and settle for a life of apathy and indifference. Others have been through the devastating trauma of personal or family illness or loss. Life hasn't turned out the way they planned or expected, the dream has become a nightmare, and they are disillusioned.

Some others are living with a continual, ongoing, low grade grief that is barely beneath the surface. They are mourning dead marriages, relationships, expectations, dreams, hopes, and goals for the future. Some are mourning dead children or the children that they longed for, and had planned to have, but never did. Others are mourning the death of their vision of the future; and yet others are mourning the gap between where they are, and where they had hoped, prayed, believed, and expected to be at this time in their lives. Over time, years of hoping and waiting, with nothing to show for it, takes a toll, and they lay down their expectancy, dreams and desires for the future. The harsh reality sets in, the fire goes out, and only the pain remains. Proverbs 13:12 says it well, "Hope deferred makes the heart sick".

Overall, the lives of many Christians is like a cemetery, with so much unfulfilled potential. This is why some people can go from a happy smile and laughter to deep painful sobs in a matter of minutes. Hidden beneath the smiles and Christian clichés is latent grief, pain, and tears over buried dreams. As soon as you breach the cemetery, the grief erupts and spills out through their eyes. Some Christian women have laid down their desire and expectancy to be mothers, because it's too late now, their biological clock has run out and they can't have children anymore. It's like something inside them, that passionate desire to be a mom, dies and is buried, and they move forward, with a dispassionate, unattached, outlook on life. They have smiles on their faces, but their hearts are heavy. For some, they have wept so much that they have no more tears. Eventually, they make peace with their circumstances, adjust their expectations, douse their fire, and live detached.

Dying Embers

When the fire goes out, embers remain. Embers are the glowing coal or wood in a dying fire. It is live and smoldering, but not ablaze. It is hot enough to scald you, but not enough to keep you warm. It has no more flames and is surrounded by ashes. Dying embers can keep water lukewarm, but not hot. It cannot heat up a house, cook food, or crackle. With more wood, fuel, accelerant, and oxygen, it can be fanned back into a roaring fire. But if left untended, it will die out completely, leaving nothing in its wake but ashes.

Unfortunately, this is the emotional address where many Christians live, among the ashes. They are surrounded by ashes of dead and dying relationships, hopes, and expectations. They love God and are committed to living for Him. They go to church regularly and serve in various capacities. They are hot, but not on fire. They believe the promises of God, but would not go out on a limb in faith. What if God doesn't come through? They know the Bible is true, but are not sure it will work for their particular situation. They believe God can do all things, but are not sure He will do it for them. They know God answers prayers, but they have unanswered prayers of their own which keeps a lid on their fire, and keeps them from bursting into flames. In one word, many Christians are lukewarm. This grieves the heart of God, who wants His people, all His people, to be on-fire. He does not want haphazard and half-hearted devotion. He is a passionate and zealous God, and created us with tremendous capacity for passion, drive, and zeal.

God cannot stand lukewarm commitments, expressions, or manifestations. In Revelation 3:15-16, He sharply rebuked the church in Laodicea for being "neither hot nor cold." Then He made a most remarkable statement. He said "I wish that you were either cold or hot. So then, because you are lukewarm and neither cold nor hot, I will spit you out of my mouth." This scripture is amazing. It is saying that God will much rather have a person who is cold spiritually, before He will choose a lukewarm Christian. He would much rather have a person who does not know or profess Christ, than a person who professes faith in Christ, but lacks any fire, passion, and zeal. The first person He will welcome and love, the second person He will abhor, and spit out of His mouth.

This is so different from the way our society has conjured up things. We have been made to believe that, "a little bit of Jesus" is better than none. If we just add a little bit of Jesus to our lifestyle, speech, hobbies, relationships, preoccupations, and week, then we are good to go. How utterly wrong! Jesus will be Lord of all, or not Lord at all. He says, "You must not have any other god but me" (Exodus 20:3). And in Isaiah 42:8 He states, "My glory I will not give to another". God requires all Christians to be fully devoted and on fire for Him.

God's Holiness

God is called "holy" more than He is called anything else in the Bible. In Isaiah 6, we see a glimpse of how holy our God is. Isaiah saw a vision of God sitting on His throne, surrounded by His court. Attending Him were mighty Seraphim, each having six wings. With two wings they covered their faces, with two they covered their feet, and with two they flew. They were constantly calling out to each other, "Holy, holy, holy is the Lord of Heaven's armies! The whole earth is filled with His glory!" (Isaiah 6:1-3).

The cry of the Seraphim is not a scripted cry. It is an exclamation, a spontaneous reaction to the utter and indescribable holiness of Almighty God. It is their unvarnished response to what they behold, a God who is so flawlessly holy. When Isaiah saw this, his reaction was equally telling. He said "It's all over! I am doomed, for I am a sinful man. I have filthy lips, and I live among a people with filthy lips." God's holiness evoked a similar response in both Isaiah and the Seraphim. The only difference was that the Seraphim did not have a conviction of sin, like Isaiah did. Isaiah was immediately convicted and instinctively knew that he could not approach or stand before this thrice holy God.

In Revelation 4:6-8, we get another glimpse into the throne room of God. We see the four living beings. The first was like a lion; the second like an ox; the third had a human face; and the fourth was like an eagle in flight. Each of these living beings had six wings, and their wings were covered all over with eyes, inside and out. Day after day and night after night they keep on saying,

> "Holy, holy, holy is the Lord God, the Almighty—
> the one who always was, who is, and who is still to come."

Here again, we see another part of the heavenly court, the four living beings. They too, like the Seraphims cry continually day and night, holy, holy, holy is the Lord God. The Seraphims and the living beings could have cried, love, love, love; or they could have cried powerful, powerful, powerful. They could have cried out any one of the awesome and innumerable qualities that personify and set our God apart. Why is it, that of all the many glorious attributes of God, the one that evokes the cry of the heavenly beings is His holiness?

John McArthur explains, "The holiness of God is not to be conceived of as one attribute among others. It is rather a general term representing the conception of God's consummate perfection and total glory. It is His infinite moral perfection crowning His infinite intelligence and power". McArthur then quotes Thomas Watson who said, "Holiness is the most sparkling jewel of God's crown, it is the name by which He is known"; and R.L. Dabney who said, "Holiness is to be regarded not as a distinct attribute, but as the result of all God's moral perfection together". In other words, Holiness is God's total glory crowned.

Speaking of God, Exodus 15:11 asks rhetorically, "Who is like you, majestic in holiness." First Samuel 2:2 says, "There is none holy as the Lord, there is none beside you". In the Bible, the term holiness is applied to God in two senses. First, God is separate, a cut above, and set apart from all that is created; and second, things are made or become holy because of their connection with God, for example, holy ground, of holy of holies. God's holiness permeates anything touched by or connected to Him.

> *Holiness is God's total glory crowned.*

In sum, God's holiness is the all-consuming, purifying perfection that sanctifies and makes holy, anything that comes in contact with Him. So, because God is distinctly holy, and He created us to have fellowship with Him, He knows that unholiness will separate us from Him, hence the clear directive to be holy because without holiness we will not "see" or fellowship with God.

The Zeal of The Lord

Zeal is an attribute that we ordinarily associate with humans. People who are driven, are seen as zealous and those who have a fervent commitment to a cause are called zealots. However, the Bible states clearly that God is zealous. In other words, God is "on-fire". Again, and again, the scripture affirms, seals and confirms a prophecy with this declaration, "the zeal of the Lord of Hosts will perform it"; meaning that God will passionately pursue and vigorously execute that prophecy, to bring it to pass. In Isaiah 9, the prophet Isaiah, after proclaiming the birth of Jesus and describing His many roles, rule and authority, states in verse 7: "Of the increases of his government and peace there shall be no end, upon the throne of David, and upon his kingdom, to order it, and to establish it with judgment and with justice from henceforth even forever. *The zeal of the Lord of Hosts will perform this".*

What is the Zeal of the Lord?

The zeal of the Lord is a holy fire that is heaven-birthed; a righteous indignation and holy anger, a burning passion for righteousness, integrity, truth and right. The zeal of the Lord is His passion. In Acts 1:3, Jesus's suffering and crucifixion is described as His "passion". "It is a spirit-empowered, heaven-enforcing, devil-crushing anointing that will break the yokes…." (Alger). It is the "display of all the divine energy and almighty omnipotence, to accomplish His purpose, to carry out His plan" (Spurgeon). The zeal of the Lord is revealed and put on display through the manifestations of the character of God.

1. **God's Zeal Displayed Through Perseverance:** We see the zeal of a person when a purpose has been in his/her heart and s/he has followed it through over a long period of time. In the same way, the zeal of God is demonstrated through His determined purpose and the inexhaustible, infinite commitment in the mind of God to bring it to pass. The plan of redemption through Jesus Christ was in the heart of God from the beginning of time. In Genesis 3:15, He promised that "the seed of the woman would bruise the serpent's head" and in Revelation 13:8, Jesus is described as "the Lamb slain from the foundation of the world". Through the eons of time, never once did the divine will waver or turn away from this set purpose. He displayed indescribable zeal when He pushed through every obstacle,

human sin and failure, and through thousands of years to bring about the birth, life, death, crucifixion and resurrection of Jesus. As Isaiah 9:6-7 prophesied over seven hundred years prior, "the zeal of the Lord of Hosts" performed it. The zeal of the Lord empowers us to persevere.

2. **God's Zeal Displayed Through Holiness and Sanctification:** In John 2:13-17, when Jesus made a whip and drove money changers out of the temple, His zealous cleansing of the temple prompted His disciples to remember and apply to Him the prophecy from the scriptures, "zeal for God's house will consume me." That righteous indignation and holy anger that burned in His spirit and moved Him to take action to cleanse the temple is the zeal of the Lord. He could not allow the temple of God to be made unclean and to become a den of thieves. The zeal of the Lord produces holiness and sanctification.

3. **God's Zeal Displayed Through Compassion:** The zeal of the Lord is a holy fire laden with compassion and mercy. It is a zeal for the salvation of souls (Isaiah 37:32). It is a ground for hope, confidence and ultimate victory. In Isaiah 63:15, the prophet declared: Lord, look down from heaven; look from your holy, glorious home, and see us. Where is the zeal, passion and the strength you used to show on our behalf? Where are your mercy and compassion now?" According to C. H. Spurgeon, this scripture "Is a battering ram with which to shake the very gates of heaven! Men of prayer and faith, learn how to use this! .....here is the

master plea, "where is your zeal, and the sounding of your heart?" The zeal of the Lord moves us with compassion.

4. **God's Zeal Displayed Through Warfare:** The zeal of the Lord's stirs Him up to war against and vanquish His enemies. Whatever challenge threatens the work of the kingdom, whatever temporary defeat appears to stop its advance, we have a sure word of prophesy, when it's all over, we win! Why? Because the zeal of the Lord of Hosts will perform it. The gates of hell shall not prevail. Isaiah 42:13 states: "The Lord shall go forth like a mighty man; He shall stir up His zeal like a man of war. He shall cry out, yes shout aloud; He shall prevail against His enemies. The zeal of the Lord gives us victory!

C. H. Spurgeon sums it up nicely, "God is not as we are—cold, insensible. He is full of zeal! And in the great good old cause, which shall, at last, win the day, there may be zealous partisans, but none is so zealous as the Lord of Hosts! A Master in the midst of Israel!" "As in the days of battle, when the front ranks are beaten, and one rank after another is driven back, up comes the old guards—and they never quail and know not how to say retreat—and so they win the day! Now behold a greater than all the hosts of men, the eternal ages, the Ancient of days, the infinite, Himself, shall bring up His servants in the day of battle! And He shall thunder gloriously! The gospel shall be proclaimed! The kingdom shall be won! Christ shall reign and the "Hallelujah" shall come up unto the Lord omnipotent, who not only gets the kingdom, but gets it by His own power, wins by His own zeal! The LORD of hosts, the LORD of hosts shall perform this".

God wants us to be zealous. The zeal of God enables us to be like God, holy, compassionate, long suffering and victorious. The zeal of God is holy fire, blazing in our hearts with passion, commitment and spiritual fervor. This zeal empowers us to stand up and speak up against an ungodly culture, and turns us into men and women with a divine mandate and assignment to impact our world for the kingdom of God. The zeal of the Lord equips us to win in all of life's battles.

Restoration of Holy Fire

Every Christian can and should be on fire for God. This chapter has outlined the many challenges and life circumstances that can beset, attack and quench the fire of God in our hearts. But we must not let it! The fire of God is precious! It is to be jealously guarded and faithfully tended in our lives. We must not let the fire go out. In 2 Timothy 1:6, apostle Paul challenged Timothy to "fan into flames the spiritual gift God gave you when I laid my hands on you". This reminder acknowledges the reality that we need to tend the fire of God in our lives and when it begins to burn low, fan it into roaring flames.

God has invested so much in His sons and daughters. We must contend earnestly for the treasure that He has put in us. "We are like fragile clay jars containing this great treasure. This makes clear that our great power is from God, not from ourselves" (2 Corinthians

4:7). So, to maintain and manifest this treasure within us, we must cultivate the presence of God. We must restore holy fire in our lives. How do we do that?

1. **Lay it Down:** Present before God, as a sacrificial offering, your deepest unfulfilled desire as a Christian. Whether it is the desire for healing, family restoration, salvation of loved ones, and so on, offer it to God, the same way Abraham offered Isaac. When we lay our deepest desires before God as a sacrifice, it is:
   a. A declaration of His Lordship over us.

   b. Confirmation that He is the primary focus of our lives.

   c. Evidence of our surrender to His will and plan for our lives.

   d. An affirmation of our trust in Him and His love and care for us.

   e. Declaration of our submission to His timing.

   f. An act of worship. When we lay our deepest desires on the altar, it is consecrated to the Lord, and the fire of God will fall and consume that sacrifice.

   g. Disarms the devil, who always tries to drive a wedge between us and God, using unfulfilled desires. When we offer our unfulfilled desires to God, the devil loses the battle. When we say like Job "Though He slay me, yet will I trust Him" (Job 13:15), the devil loses his ability to use our unfulfilled desires to slander God to us.

2. **Get Up and Out:** Stop rehearsing your disappointments and failures, that will only lead to resentment. Recognize that what happened to you explains why you are where you are, but is no reason for you to stay there. Determine in your heart to get up and out. This does not mean that you can snap your fingers and "be happy". What it does mean is that the Holy Spirit can execute the divine exchange described in Isaiah 61:1-3. He can take your ashes and give you His beauty, exchange your spirit of grief and mourning, with His joy; and help you to put on the garment of praise when the spirit of heaviness tries to overtake you. Note that praise is a garment, and so, you have to put it on; just like your clothes don't just "jump on you", but you have to put them on. So, when the spirit of grief and heaviness tries to come upon you, you have to make a conscious choice to put on the garment of praise, by turning on praise music, singing, and thanking God. Though at the outset, you may still feel downcast, as you continue to praise God, you will pierce the darkness of depression, mount up with wings like an eagle and soar on the wings of praise above the bitterness and heaviness of your disappointments.

> *Hope is a confident expectation that God will do what He said He will do.*

3. **Rekindle Hope:** Hope is a confident expectation that God will do what He said He will do. Has God made you a promise? Have you been standing on the word of God for a long time? Do you feel disappointed and discouraged? I challenge you to rekindle your hope. Do not cast away your confidence. God will keep His word to you. He made an appointment with you when He gave you His word, and He will keep that appointment, no matter what.

4. **Take Responsibility:** Own your part in creating the disappointments you have experienced. Let me explain. It is the weight that we attach to anything that gives it the power to disappoint and crush us. Reassess your own value system and challenge how much value you attach to the things that have disappointed and disillusioned you. This does not mean that you stop wanting those things, but it does mean that you surrender the timing, anxiety and worry about them to the Lord, and leave it there. It's like the apostle Paul. When he became immersed in Christ, the result was a striking reassessment and shift in his value system. In Philippians 3:7-8, after recounting his pedigree, achievements and accolades in the natural, he said "I once thought these things were valuable, but now I consider them worthless because of what Christ has done. Yes, everything else is worthless when compared with the infinite value of knowing Christ Jesus my Lord. For his sake I have discarded everything else, counting it all as garbage, so that I could gain Christ and become one with him."

5. **The Word of God**: The word of God is a sure and steadfast anchor for the soul. Saturate your mind and heart with the word of God. The word of God is filled with the power of God and will rekindle holy fire in your soul. John 1:1 tells us that the word of God is Jesus Christ Himself. So, the more word you have in you, the more Jesus you have in you. Filling your mind with the word of God will shift your perspective, permeate your psyche, reshape and supplant your worldview; and you will see yourself through His eyes. The Word of God is filled with the Zoë life of God and will fill you with abundant life.

6. **Fasting and Prayer**: Seeking God in fasting and prayer will rekindle your fire and drench your soul with His refreshing. There is nothing quite like spending time alone with God to renew your strength, rekindle your fire and clarify your focus. When my soul is frazzled, discontented, distracted and disquieted within me, I step away and spend time seeking the face of the Lord. Every single time, the Lord is my reward. When I bask in His presence, He saturates my being with Himself, quietens my heart and confirms my faith and trust in His working and timing in my life.

> *Victory comes when you say the same thing about yourself, that God says about you!*

7. **Proclaim the Word:** The spoken word of God is our offensive weapon. It is the sword of the Spirit. Revelation 12:11 states, "And they overcame him by the blood of the Lamb and by the word of their testimony". In Mark 11:23,

Jesus said, "I say to you, whoever says to this mountain, 'Be removed and be cast into the sea,' and does not doubt in his heart, but believes that those things he says will be done, he will have whatever he says." You cannot overestimate the power of the spoken word. This is how we fight our battles. This is how we win! So, to restore holy fire, take the word of God in your mouth and speak it forth. Victory comes when you say the same thing about yourself, that God says about you!

8. **Trust in God's Plan and Timing**: When your heart gets weary from waiting, remind yourself that God knows you by name, sees you, knows exactly where you are and hears the cry of your heart. Affirming your trust in God will rekindle holy fire in your soul. God cares personally, intimately and passionately for you. Remind yourself that not even one sparrow falls to the ground without our heavenly Father's notice. You are much more valuable that many sparrows. God has you on His mind twenty four hours a day; so much so, that He has numbered the hairs on your head. Psalm 139:17-18 states, "How precious are your thoughts about me, O God. They cannot be numbered! I can't even count them; they outnumber the grains of sand! And when I wake up, you are still with me!" You are always on the mind of God. He is constantly thinking about you.

Second Chronicles 16:9 states, "For the eyes of the Lord run to and fro throughout the whole earth to show Himself strong on behalf of those whose heart is loyal to Him". If you have been waiting long for God, don't grow weary. God is mightily at work on your behalf. Isaiah 64:4 states, "For since the world began no ear has heard and no eye has seen a God like you, who works for those who wait for him!" One of the names of God that is not in the Bible is Jehovah nick of time. God often comes, just in the nick of time. He is never in a hurry, but He is never late. He will come at the right time and will perfect all that concerns you – Amen.

9. **Find Purpose Beyond Yourself, Invest Yourself in Others**: One sure fire way to rekindle the fire of God in your heart, is to take your eyes off of yourself and become "others focused". Helping other people never fails to heal, restore and give you a fresh sense of purpose. Focusing on yourself and what you don't have, is not only depressing, it can lead to ingratitude and an obsession. That territory is the devil's stomping ground. Regardless of what is not presently in your life today, there is always so much that you have to be thankful for. Helping others reminds you of how blessed you are, and helps you to remember to give thanks for what you do have. When you help others, you multiply joy by giving joy to others. When you sow joy, you will reap joy. When you help someone else overcome today, you have a sense of purpose and blessing that reinvigorates you. God created you to be a blessing, so blessing others gives you a sense of wellbeing, because it fulfills one of your primary assignments and purposes on earth.

The Power of a Personal Altar

It is impossible to be on-fire for God without a personal altar. In fact, an altar-less Christian is a powerless Christian. To restore holy fire in your life, you must have an altar where the fire of God will fall. An altar is a time and/or place that is sanctified or set apart for God. It is a time and/or place where you meet with God. In Exodus 20:23-24, God said to the Children of Israel, "Remember, you must not make any idols of silver or gold to rival me. Build for me an altar made of earth. Build my altar wherever I cause my name to be remembered, and I will come to you and bless you."

Here God is saying, if you want to meet with me, don't make an image, raise an altar. Altars are very significant in spiritual warfare. It is a gateway into the supernatural. If you prepare and set apart a time and/or place to meet with and seek God, you are most likely to have divine encounters at that time or place. An altar is a place of invocation. It is a place of activation or servicing of covenants. It is a place of worship, sacrifice, blessing, refuge, and protection (Exodus 20:24;1 Kings 1:50-53; 2:28-29).

> *An altar-less Christian is a powerless Christian.*

Under the Old Testament, people raised physical stone altars. Abraham raised several altars to the Lord. So did Isaac and Jacob (Genesis 28:1-22). Under the New Testament, believers in Jesus are themselves the temples of God and our heart is His altar (Corinthians 6:19-2). So, to set up a personal altar, all you need to do is to establish a time and/or place, consecrate it to the Lord, make a commitment to the Lord to meet with Him there, and then, follow through and show up at that time or place.

Blessings of the Altar

There are many blessings of a personal altar. A Christian with a personal altar will experience progressive brokenness, holiness, and consecration. By setting up an altar, you are saying, Lord, I give you my full attention. God in turn responds in the words of Jeremiah 29:13, "If you seek me, you will find me when you search for me with all your heart". When you raise an altar, it is an invitation to God, and He always shows up.

An altar is a declaration of dependence on God and an acknowledgment of His ownership and Lordship over your life. It cultivates the presence of God, and an ability to hear, and recognize His voice. Altars sharpen spiritual perception and discernment (Romans 12:2; Acts 16:16-19). It is a place to receive divine guidance, and for the manifestation of the power of God (1 Kings 18:30-39). For the New Testament Christian, an altar is a place to activate, appropriate, and deploy the finished works of Christ!

Several years ago, I heard a story that illustrated, so strongly, the power of a personal altar. It is the story of a young ruffian who gave his life to Christ. This guy was a member of a motorcycle gang, and was into all manner of drugs, sin, and debauchery. His body was a walking billboard of tattoos. He was a rude, crude, leud, dude. Then he met Jesus. He did not have a Christian background and had never been to church. He worked a construction job, and there was a little old church near the construction job site. So, every afternoon at lunch time, he would go to the church. The first time he went there, he turned the knob, and the door opened. He walked in and sat down towards the back. Nobody was there. He fidgeted a little, cleared his throat a couple times and awkwardly said, "Jesus, man, I think you are cool. I just want to say, it's really been great knowing you". He didn't know what else to say, so, he sat for a little while longer, and left. Every day at lunch time, he would make his trip to the church to talk to Jesus. Unbeknownst to him, the pastor of the church had been observing him from the vestry. The first time he came, the pastor was afraid, and wondered whether he had come to steal or perpetrate some felony at the church. But after he came for a couple times, the pastor approached him, introduced himself, chatted with him for a while and heard the young man's story about how he had lived the life of a prodigal and how Jesus saved him. He told him he was welcome at the church anytime.

After a while, the young man stopped coming. A week passed, and the pastor got curious. So, he went to the construction site to inquire, and found out that the young man had fallen from a scaffolding and was in the hospital. The pastor went to visit him. When he came into his hospital room, he saw a chair pulled up against the bed, like someone had been visiting. He knew from his discussion with the young man that his lifestyle had alienated his family, and he was estranged from his parents. It was unlikely that anybody would visit him in the hospital. So, he asked him, "looks like you've had visitors?" The young man with tears in his eyes told the pastor that every day, at lunch time, Jesus came to visit and sat in that Chair. He would call him by name and say to him, "man, I think you are cool. I just want to say, it's really been great knowing you".

This is the power of a personal altar. It brings the presence of God. The young man did not know it, but he had set up a personal altar with the Lord, and when he couldn't come to the church, Jesus kept that appointment and came to him in the hospital. The rest of the story is that while his accident was very serious, and he had been expected to die or have permanent disability from his fall, he was miraculously healed by the love and grace of God.

The Fellowship of the Unashamed

Are you on-fire for God? If not, are you ready for the restoration of holy fire in your life? Are you all-in and sold out, or do you have a plan B? Are you a follower or a fan? Are you a disciple of Jesus Christ? Are you part of the fellowship of the unashamed?

A Rwandan man in 1980 was being forced by his tribe to either renounce Christ or face certain death. He refused to renounce Christ, and was killed on the spot. The night before, he had written a personal commitment "The Fellowship of the Unashamed", which was later found in his room. Since then, this declaration has been adopted by and has become the creed of Christians who are all-in and on-fire for Christ. If that describes you, then read this, let it sink into your soul and become your personal declaration of commitment.

>I am part of the "Fellowship of the Unashamed."
>
>The die has been cast. I have stepped over the line.

The decision has been made. I am a disciple of Jesus Christ. I won't look back, let up, slow down, back away, or be still. My past is redeemed, my present makes sense, and my future is secure. I am finished and done with low living, sight walking, small planning, smooth knees, colorless dreams, chintzy giving, and dwarfed goals.

I no longer need preeminence, prosperity, position, promotions, plaudits, or popularity. I now live by presence, lean by faith, love by patience, lift by prayer, and labor by power. My pace is set, my gait is fast, my goal is Heaven, my road is narrow, my way is rough, my companions few, my Guide reliable, my mission clear. I cannot be bought, compromised, deterred, lured away, turned back, diluted, or delayed.

I will not flinch in the face of sacrifice, hesitate in the presence of adversity, negotiate at the table of the enemy, ponder at the pool of popularity, or meander in the maze of mediocrity.

I am a disciple of Jesus Christ. I must go until Heaven returns, give until I drop, preach until all know, and work until He comes. And when He comes to get His own, He will have no problem recognizing me. My colors will be clear.

As I wrote this chapter, Holy Spirit brought to my memory a short chorus written long ago by Rosemary Hilvers. When I was a teenager, I sang this song with deep conviction, as a declaration of my passionate commitment to Christ. I challenge you to speak the words of this song as a prayer over yourself, make it your personal declaration and regularly proclaim it over yourself.

> The zeal of God has consumed me
> It burns within my soul
> A driving force that cannot be stopped
> A fire that cannot be quenched

Present yourself to the Lord and consecrate your life to Him. His holy fire will fall and set your heart ablaze.

How to Successfully Engage Your Season!

How you engage this season of your life will determine the outcome and impact of your life! You can spend your time feeling sorry for yourself for all the things that did not go right for you, or you can actively engage this season of your life and change your world! There are many things you can do. You can take the challenge to make your life more interesting; or seize the opportunity to make needed changes in your life; or take action to remove the wrong people from your life. You can be bold and do something you've never done before - take a class, go on a mission trip, read, travel, or volunteer to help others. The worst that can happen is that you'll become an even more interesting person and impact more people.

One thing is clear, we will give account to God for every season of our lives. In Matthew 25:14-30, Jesus told the parable of the talents. The master gave one servant, five talents; the other, two talents; and the last servant, one talent. While the servants with five and two talents worked and invested their talents, the servant with one talent went and hid his talent. He had an excuse, he was resentful against the master, but that did not exonerate him. The master's judgment was stern and His sentence swift: "He ordered, 'take the talent from this servant, and give it to the one with the ten talents. To those who use well what they are given, even more will be given, and they will have an abundance. But from those who did nothing, even what little they have will be taken away. Now throw this useless servant into outer darkness where there will be weeping and gnashing of teeth.'

> *It doesn't matter what you have, it matters only what you do with what you have.*

Sadly, this is the tale of so many Christians today. They believe that they have been given one talent. They are not as gifted as others. Others appear to have the perfect life, the life they so desperately want and pray for. Like the one talent guy, they feel resentful. They feel that life has given them a raw deal. Some feel that God has disappointed them. They have lived a good life and served God faithfully, but things didn't turn out the way they hoped. They did not expect to be where they are at this time in their lives, or for this long. Some have been through traumatic events, and they feel that those events were unfair. Maybe they prayed and believed for their family member to be healed and they died anyway, or they prayed for years for a loved one to be saved and nothing has happened.

Well, being resentful towards the master was not a good excuse for the servant in Jesus' parable, nor is it for us. You see, like that servant, God has invested so much in us. Jesus died to save us and gave us His Spirit to impact our world. Every person has at least one talent, the precious Holy Spirit living inside us, the same Spirit that raised Jesus from the dead! We can choose to make excuses or we can get to work. But one thing is sure, one day, we will be required to give an account of what we did with our lives.

> *Every Christian has the best "one talent" in the world, the precious Holy Spirit!*

The Master's Response

1. He took the talent from him and gave it to the guy who was busy. Has it ever occurred to you that God never gives anything worthwhile to anybody who is idle? In fact, every person Jesus

called, was busy working. Peter, James and John, were fishing; Matthew was collecting taxes; Simon was a zealot, and so on. It seemed that Jesus could stand just about anybody – sinners, prostitutes, tax collectors, and so on, except indolent people. He called busy people and then He gave them more work to do. We think differently. We think, give the work to the man who has nothing to do. But Jesus doesn't do that. He is interested in productive people. It doesn't matter to Him what you have, it matters only what you do with what you have. He will never ask of us what He did not give us. He said expressly to us, "occupy till I come". We must be about the master's business. God has given us gifts, talents and time. We can choose to invest or squander them. Note that the Bible says in Matthew 12:36, that we will give account for every idle word that we speak. That is how much God dislikes idleness. We will account for every idle or non-working word we speak. If we will give account for idle words, He will certainly require us to give account for unproductive lives.

2. The one talent guy did not take responsibility for his life. He did what many people do today. They blame the outcomes of their lives on someone else. Their ex-spouse, ex-boy or girl-friend, ex-boss, or on the Lord, who didn't answer their prayer. That ruse did not work for the servant and it will not work for you. As an adult, it is your responsibility to tend to your own life. It's a waste of precious time and energy to obsess over your circumstances. This is an exciting time to be alive! Determine to take your eyes off yourself, and to act on purpose, and with intentionality to impact your world and transform the lives of people in your sphere of influence. God wants

you to live a life of purpose, passion and power. He is at work in your life and all around you. Join Him!

3. Doing nothing with your talent produces bitterness and multiplies resentment. The derelict servant did nothing with his talent, so, his one talent remained one talent. At the same time, the five talent guy had grown his five talents to ten, and the two talent guy had multiplied his talents to four. Notice that the gap is widening between the one talent guy and his colleagues who were at work. Notice also that when the master returned, the derelict servant did most of the talking. He had nothing to show for his wasted years. So, he complained about the master, accused and maligned him. If the master had allowed him to continue talking, he would have moved on to the two and five talent guys; and waxed eloquent about how arrogant they were; and how they thought they were better than everybody else; and how things always worked out for them; after all, they started out with so much more than he did. That is the loser's creed. Losers take little, if any, responsibility for their lives. They disclaim responsibility for their choices and blame others. But their whining and envy does not confuse the master. He sees it for what it is. A thin cover for their laziness. Your rotten lot in life or what people did to you may be the reason why you are the way you are, but do not use it as an excuse to stay that way. Your future is your responsibility.

> *Your future is your responsibility.*

4. Think about it, if the one talent guy could not produce a profit from only one talent, how could he ever hope to be useful to the master? The scripture says that they were given talents according to their ability. The two talent guy did not bemoan his two talents, accuse

the master or envy the guy with five. He simply put his two talents to work. But the one talent guy did not. In Luke 16:10-12, Jesus taught us an important principle. "If you are unfaithful in little things, you will be unfaithful in large things. If you are dishonest in little things, you won't be honest with greater responsibilities. And if you are untrustworthy about worldly wealth, who will trust you with the true riches of heaven? And if you are unfaithful with other people's things, why should you be trusted with things of your own?"

This principle has direct application here. If you cannot manage your own life and invest your time to be productive for the kingdom of God today, why would God give you more responsibility? Many of the "blessings" we ask God for require work. For example, a great harvest is a blessing, but it requires a lot of work to bring it in. A promotion at work is a blessing, but it means more responsibility. So, why would God give you more responsibility when you have demonstrated that you are not capable of effectively managing your life and current responsibilities?

5. The one talent guy wanted to control the outcome. He had one talent, and he was afraid of the master, so he wanted to ensure that he incurred no loss. He did not want to take any risk of loss, and by ensuring no risk of loss, he also gave up the potential upside. You see, risk is like a pendulum that swings both ways. It has the downside potential for loss and pain, but it also has the upside potential for gain and increase. The problem is, there are no guarantees. Any investment requires risk. It requires giving up control. It requires effort and faith that the outcome will justify the investment. This was a bridge too far for the one talent guy. Even

though he blamed his master, the fault was much deeper and very personal. He did not have enough faith in himself to invest his talent in his own future. So, he settled for the status quo.

6. The master consigns the derelict servant to outer darkness, a place of punishment and gnashing of teeth, not because he had one talent, but because he was useless and unproductive. This is instructive. It is the same reason Jesus cursed the fig tree in Mark 11:12-14. From a distance, it was in "full leaf", giving an appearance of fruitfulness, but when Jesus came closer and looked for fruit on it, it was unproductive. It was all leaves and no fruit. We will give account to God for what we do with every season of our lives.

Invest in Eternity

By far, the greatest trust God has placed in us is the stewardship of our time. God lives in eternity, but we live in time, and God has given us stewardship of our time. Time is the most precious commodity we have. Our lives are made up of seconds and minutes. Everyone gets the exact same amount of time. Every day, we each get 24 hours to spend, invest or squander as we choose. And the next day, the same. When we go to work, we are paid for our time. Some people describe it as "putting in our time". Each paycheck is essentially payment for a portion of our lives that we will never be able to live again. We traded those hours in for cash. Same thing with the rest of our lives, some of us trade it in for worthless trifles, while others invest it for eternal impact. Take a Friday night for example. Some people will squander it on frivolous fritters, a few hours at a bar, illicit sex, gambling or some other fleeting past time; others will "kill time" with mindless television binge watching; while others will invest it in a wholesome evening with their children and family; or serving the poor and needy at a homeless shelter; or coaching young boys who do not have a dad in their lives. The same exact time, invested very differently, with very different impacts and outcomes, some trivial, and others eternal.

Our lives are meted out to us in 24 hour increments. We are not told how many 24 hour installments we will have, only to be judicious and wise in how we spend each allotment of time we get. One thing about time, once we spend it, we can never get it back. 8am of today is gone, and until I die, I will never again re-live 8am of December 7, 2021. It is gone forever, and anything I did not do at 8am today, I will never again, until I die, do it at 8am of December 7, 2021. Soon, this day will be gone forever, and all that is left are memories. One day, our time on earth will be over and there will be an obituary or cemetery somewhere that tells a short story about our lives. Typically, it will give the deceased's name, the year of their birth, a little dash, and then the year of their death. A little dash, that's all it is. Think of the brevity of it, just a little dash. That little dash is the sum total of our lives. Whether we lived a hundred years or 10 years doesn't matter. What matters is what we did with our dash. My challenge to you today is to invest your dash in serving others and building the kingdom of God.

This season of your life is a precious gift from God. Invest this time with eternity in view. Below is a poem about time that made a big impact on me. Read it, consider and ponder it, and let it motivate you to live a fruitful and productive life.

The Value of Time

Imagine there is a bank account that credits your account each morning with $86,400. It carries over no balance from day to day. Every evening the bank deletes whatever part of the balance you failed to use during the day. What would you do? Draw out every cent, of course? Each of us has such a bank. It's name is TIME. Every morning, it credits you with 86,400 seconds. Every night it writes off as lost, whatever allotment of this time you failed to invest for a good purpose. It carries over no balance. It allows no overdraft. Each day it opens a new account for you. Each night it burns the remains of the day. If you fail to use the day's deposits, the loss is yours. There is no drawing against "tomorrow." You must live in the present on today's deposits. Invest it so as to get from it the utmost in health, happiness and success!

The clock is ticking! Be diligent to make the most of today.

To realize the value of ONE YEAR, ask a student who failed a grade.
To realize the value of ONE MONTH, ask a mother who has given birth to a premature baby.
To realize the value of ONE WEEK, ask the editor of a weekly newspaper.
To realize the value of ONE HOUR, ask the lovers who are waiting to meet.
To realize the value of ONE MINUTE, ask a person who just missed a train.
To realize the value of ONE SECOND, ask someone who just avoided an accident.

To realize the value of ONE MILLISECOND, ask the person who won a silver medal at the Olympics.

Treasure every moment that you have! And remember time waits for no one. Yesterday is history. Tomorrow is a mystery. Today is a gift. That's why it's called the present.

CHAPTER 5
LOVING

The next step to living a whole and fulfilled life is love. The words love and loving are the heart of the gospel. Love is the nature of God. It is not what He does, it is who He is. First John 4:8 states very clearly that "God is love". And John 3:16 explains that, God so loved the world that He gave His only son. In John 13:34-35 Jesus said, "A new commandment I give to you, that you love one another, as I have loved you, that you also love one another. By this all will know that you are my disciples, if you have love for one another." In yet another scripture, when Jesus was asked what was the greatest commandment, his response was quick and unequivocal "You shall love the Lord your God with all your heart, with all your soul, with all your mind, and with all your strength.' This is the first commandment. And the second, like it, is this: 'You shall love your neighbor as yourself'. There is no other commandment greater than these" (Matthew 22:37).

It is abundantly clear that from God's vantage point, love is the greatest. It is at once the very nature of God, the identity badge that distinguishes disciples of Christ, and the first and greatest commandment. Love is the greatest! Amazingly, the world agrees! Everyone loves the word love. In one breath we can love ice cream, music, TV shows, our friends, spouse and God.

Love is a word that is over used, misused and abused. So, let's examine what the Bible means by love.

Love Is the Greatest

The Bible is very detailed in its explanation of what love means. First Corinthians 13 is called the love chapter because it is totally devoted to the subject of love. It starts out by establishing the supreme import of love. Love, God's kind of love, transcends and is greater than all knowledge, faith, linguistic ability, prophetic insight, power, miracles, signs and wonders. It is the only pure motive. Anything we do, say or achieve, regardless of how noble or altruistic, if it is not undergirded by biblical love, is useless, a complete waste of time, and will have no eternal impact. Eugene Peterson puts it succinctly in the Message Bible, "So, no matter what I say, what I believe, and what I do, I'm bankrupt without love" (1 Corinthians 13:4).

> First Corinthians 13:1-3 states:
> If I could speak all the languages of earth and of angels, but didn't love others, I would only be a noisy gong or a clanging cymbal. If I had the gift of prophecy, and if I understood all of God's secret plans and possessed all knowledge, and if I had such faith that I could move mountains, but didn't love others, I would be nothing. If I gave everything I have to the poor and even sacrificed my body, I could boast about it; but if I didn't love others, I would have gained nothing.

What this passage is saying is that, without love, Jesus' sacrifice on the cross would have been utterly devoid of meaning or ability to save even a single soul. Think about it, if Jesus had suffered the horrendous beating that tore his back to shreds, the mockery and humiliation of the soldiers, the murderous rage of the religious leaders, the blood lust of the militant crowd, and the derision of the thief on the cross beside him, if He endured all that for any other reason or motivation than love, it would have been utterly useless, and completely impotent to save mankind. That is how critical love is! Love goes to the heart of the matter. It asks the question why? It's not what you do, but why you do it. That is what matters most. Guess who else is focused on the heart? God. First Samuel 16:7 says: "The Lord doesn't see things the way you see them. People judge by outward appearance, but the Lord looks at the heart." Biblical love is a matter of the heart.

Biblical Love

Biblical love is not a feeling. It is a choice, a decision, a commitment and an action. Biblical love is not google-eyed fantasy or day dreaming about rainbows and dew drops. It is love in working clothes, it is dirty, it is smelly, it is costly, and it is others focused. Most of all, it is practical. It does not stand by idly and make grandiose claims of affection. It is not loud, boisterous or effusive. It is not all mouth. Rather, it gives you a practical yardstick with which to measure your actions, reactions, perspectives and attitudes. It challenges your motives, encourages your perseverance and demands your allegiance.

Years ago, I was challenged by a mentor, to read 1 Corinthians 13 in an introspective way. She challenged me to locate everywhere that the word love occurred in the chapter, and to substitute my name in its place. I did and what a scathing rebuke that was! As I read and re-read the personalized chapter, I realized that, whereas I had previously felt "love", been "in love", and told friends and relatives that I loved them, my definition of love was flawed and far different from the biblical definition.

> First Corinthians 13:4-7 states: Love is patient and kind. Love is not jealous or boastful or proud or rude. It does not demand its own way. It is not irritable, and it keeps no record of being wronged. It does not rejoice about injustice but rejoices whenever the truth wins out. Love never gives up, never loses faith, is always hopeful, and endures through every circumstance.

So, if you are impatient and unkind in your treatment of people; if you are jealous or proud; if your speech is rude and laced with sarcasm; if you are demanding, self-willed, and it's your way or the highway; if you are obnoxious, bristling, brusque, and curt; and if you have a long memory of past wrongs; I don't care how you feel, you do not exhibit God's love.

I was convicted. The Holy Spirit showed me that my impatience was a manifestation of pride. I had an exalted view of myself, and did not think that I should wait on or for others. He also pointed out that my impatience made me rude and irritable. Also, the Holy Spirit convicted me of my insistence on "my right". Months earlier, a distant relative had spread really negative and untrue gossip about me and my family. It was very hurtful. Not too long after that, they were exposed, not only for the untruth they told about my family, but about others as well. Other character issues and flaws about them surfaced, and they were publicly humiliated. I rejoiced at my "vindication". But there and then, the Holy Spirit rebuked me. He told me that love does not rejoice in the wrong. He directed me to pray for this person, for genuine conviction, repentance, healing and restoration. That, is the love of God, it is a love that is beyond us and that looks out for the best interest of the other person. Biblical love is eternal, because God is love.

> *Biblical love is not a feeling. It is a choice, a decision, a commitment and an action.*

Types of Love in the Bible

Four unique forms of love are found in the Bible. They are expressed in the Greek words – Eros, Storge, Philia and Agape.

1. **Eros** is the Greek word for sensual or romantic love. The term originated from the mythological Greek god Eros, the god of love, sexual desire, physical attraction and physical love.

2. **Storge** is the Greek word that describes family love, the natural affection between parents and children, brothers and sisters, and so on. This is the word used to describe the love Martha and Mary had for their brother Lazarus.

3. **Philia** is the Greek word that describes brotherly love. The strong emotional bond of friendship, care, respect and compassion for other people. This is the root word from which

we derive the name Philadelphia, the city of brotherly love. And, this is the love that Jesus, in John 13:35, said is the identifying mark of every disciple.

4. **Agape** is the Greek word that describes the highest form of love in the Bible. It is God's immeasurable, inexhaustible, incomparable love for human beings. "Agape love is perfect, unconditional, sacrificial and pure." This word was used by Jesus when He, after His resurrection, asked Peter three times if he loved Him. Peter replied that he did, but the word he used was philia. So, Jesus asked Peter, "Do you agape me?" And Peter responds, "Yes I philia you."

Loving

Christians are created, commanded and equipped to love. We have a tremendous God-given capacity and divine enablement to act in a loving way, regardless of how we feel. Romans 5:5 states that "God has given us the Holy Spirit to fill our hearts with His love". So, we have the capacity to love like God loves. This capacity is deposited within us by the Holy Spirit when we receive Jesus as our savior. But we must choose to exercise or demonstrate this love.

> *People who don't love themselves, devalue and mistreat others.*

Loving Yourself

In Matthew 22:34-40, the Bible records that a Pharisee, an expert in religious law, tried to trap Jesus with a question. "Teacher, which is the most important commandment in the law of Moses? Jesus replied, "You must love the Lord your God with all your heart, all your soul, and all your mind. This is the first and greatest commandment. A second is equally important: "Love your neighbor as yourself".

In His response, Jesus quoted the first of the ten commandments that God gave to Moses on Mount Sinai. That is unquestionably, the greatest commandment. Then He added to it a second commandment from Leviticus 19:18; "love your neighbor as yourself"; elevated this second commandment, and made it comparable to the first.

The second commandment has a premise "as yourself". It assumes or infers that you love yourself, and then tells you to love others, in the same way. Loving yourself is therefore foundational to your capacity to love others. If you do not love yourself, you cannot truly love others. This biblical truth, has been validated again and again by human experience. Hurting people hurt people. People who don't love themselves, devalue and mistreat others.

Loving yourself means recognizing that God is the I AM that I AM and that His I AM image is in you. It is knowing that your identity is in Christ and Christ alone. Loving yourself means caring for your body and investing your life to make a difference. It means leaving a legacy and making every day of your life count. Loving yourself includes loving the people in your life, letting go of the past, the guilt, condemnation and mistakes, and believing God for a new beginning. It means forgiving yourself and not being tethered to fear, worry and anxiety. Loving yourself means finding your purpose in life, and doing that thing or the things that bring you joy and deep personal satisfaction. Ladies, it means taking some "me time" to get your nails done, get a massage, buy yourself a gift, or hang out with your friends without feeling guilty about the kids. For the guys, it can be taking a day off to enjoy fishing, golf or other sport activity you enjoy. Simply stated, loving yourself means living an abundant life, the life that Jesus came to give to us.

Often in today's society, you see two extremes. At one extreme are the people who do not love themselves. Some of these people do not even like themselves - how they look, the work they do, who they are, and so on. They do not value themselves and routinely put themselves down. Others are ashamed of themselves, their background, what they've done, and their past failures and mistakes. They sometimes falsely think that humility requires self-deprecation, and so they denigrate, discount and devalue themselves.

Keep in mind that having a healthy dose of self-knowledge that acknowledges your quirks, recognizes your failures and mistakes, and allows you to laugh at yourself, is an important aspect of humility and being a happy and fulfilled person. But these people take it to an extreme.

At the other extreme are individuals who are narcissistic. The word narcissism comes from a Greek myth about Narcissus, a man who "sees his own reflection in a pool of water and falls in love with it". Narcissists have an exaggerated view of their own importance. They think and talk often about themselves, lack empathy and have little regard for others. They have elaborate fantasies about the future, and feel that they should have the best of everything. Narcissists feel superior to and belittle others to maintain their feeling of superiority. Despite their outward portrayal of confidence, they are grossly insecure and have a fragile self-esteem. So, they require constant praise and admiration to prop themselves up. They have a sense of entitlement, think that others exist to serve their own needs, and take advantage of others.

Here again, while possessing a sense of personal importance and uniqueness are important aspects of being a happy and fulfilled person, narcissists take it to an extreme.

Knowing Yourself

Loving yourself starts with knowing yourself. Knowing yourself means understanding your temperament, strengths and weaknesses, passions and fears, desires and dreams. It means being aware of your eccentricities and idiosyncrasies, your likes and dislikes, your preferences and potential, and your tolerances and limitations. Knowing yourself means discovering your unique personal foundation, definition, and authenticity.

Why is Self-Knowledge Important?

Thales of Miletus once said, "The most difficult thing in life is to know yourself". However, good things come to those who invest in this enterprise.

1. **Confidence:** You will be happier and more confident when you can express who you are with some certainty. Also, knowing your likes and dislikes, and being able to articulate and express them will help you achieve them.

2. **Personal Authenticity:** Knowing yourself allows your outward actions to correspond to or be in alignment with your inner self and core values. It supports personal authenticity and reduces internal conflict.

3. **Better Decision Making:** When you know your core values, likes, dislikes and preferred outcomes, it supports better decision making. Self-knowledge eliminates self-doubt, promotes decisive internal dialogue and provides the framework for better decision making.

4. **Self-Control:** Knowing yourself, your appetites, propensities, preferences, proclivities and bents, gives you tremendous personal insight and self-control. You become self-aware. You know how you tend to react in various situations, what motivates you, ticks you off and sets you up or off. Self-knowledge empowers you to say "no" to yourself, the devil, sin and the world, and it helps you to make wise choices and say "yes" to God.

5. **Empathy & Grace**: Self-knowledge makes you less critical and judgmental of others. You are able to empathize with the failures, weaknesses and frailties of other people. You are able to give grace and mercy to people because you can truly say with understanding, "There, but for the grace of God, go I".

6. **Empowerment**: Knowing who you are empowers you to live life to the full. It promotes self-acceptance and empowerment. You know your limitations and failures, but you also know your strengths and abilities. Knowing yourself helps you to be comfortable in your own skin. It empowers you to change what needs to change, and accept what you cannot change about yourself.

7. **Celebrate Yourself**: Self-knowledge helps you to celebrate yourself as you are. A biblically based self-assessment promotes personal approval, personal value and contentment. It helps you affirm your capabilities, own your strengths, pursue your dreams and celebrate your accomplishments.

8. **Promotes Purpose:** Knowing yourself helps you to hone in on your purpose. You don't waste time in trivial pursuits, interests or activities that do not contribute to your purpose. It helps you to identify where you belong and to minimize distractions. Knowing yourself helps you identify what it important to you, so you can focus on achieving it. It helps you prioritize and not allow people to clog your life and schedule with their interests and agenda.

> *Knowing yourself means discovering the core building blocks of self that make you, you.*

The Building Blocks of Self

Knowing yourself includes discovering the distinctive attributes that define you and the core building blocks of self that make you, you. These include:

1. Temperament

A lot has been written about temperaments. Dr. Tim LaHaye's book, *Spirit Controlled Temperament,* is an excellent resource on this topic. In it, he defines temperament as, "The combination of inborn traits that subconsciously affects all our behavior. These traits, which are passed on by our genes, are based on hereditary factors and arranged at the time of conception"

There are five basic temperaments, the choleric, sanguine, phlegmatic, melancholy, and supine, and over four thousand temperament blends.

> **1. Choleric** is the hot, quick, active, practical and strong willed temperament. Cholerics are driven, self-sufficient, and fiercely independent. They are self-starters, goal oriented, practical, and capable of making sound decisions. Cholerics are born leaders. They are quick to recognize and take advantage of opportunities, have a dogged determination, and often succeed where others fail. However, Cholerics lack empathy, mercy, and compassion, and love is often not high on their list of priorities. Because Cholerics can achieve so much, they often have no sympathy for those who can't. In the Bible, apostle Paul was a choleric.

2. Sanguine is the warm, buoyant, lively and fun loving temperament. Sanguines are extroverts and the life of the party. For them, feelings rather than reflective thoughts predominate in decision formation. The sanguine is never at a loss for words, though s/he often speaks without thinking. Sanguines are not very organized and can readily forget appointments, responsibilities and obligations. They can be noisy, blustery, friendly, energetic and lovable. In the Bible, apostle Peter was a Sanguine.

3. Phlegmatic is the calm, cool, easygoing and well balanced temperament. S/He has a very high boiling point and never seems to be ruffled or angry. Phlegmatics are very consistent and keep their emotions under control. They enjoy people, have a dry sense of humor, and are quite adept at avoiding as much involvement as possible. They are reluctant leaders, but when roused into action, they are very competent and passionate. Phlegmatics are not risktakers. They are well organized, work well under pressure and are very dependable. Abraham was a phlegmatic.

4. Melancholy is the analytical, self-sacrificing, gifted, perfectionist, with a very sensitive, emotional nature. Melancholics are introverts and can be moody. They do not make friends easily, but when made, are very loyal and faithful. They are very dependable, thorough and precise, and their exceptional analytical abilities enable them to accurately diagnose the pitfalls of any project. Melancholics tend to have high IQ, creativity and imagination. They often find their greatest meaning in life through sacrifice, and can choose a difficult life vocation, involving great personal cost. No temperament has as much natural potential when energized by the Holy Spirit as the Melancholy. Apostle John was a melancholic.

5. Supine is the quiet, very accommodating, "loves to serve" temperament. Supines are both introverted and extroverted, have a servant's heart, appear to be withdrawn and are often in the background. They like people, have a great capacity for service, and possess an inborn gentle spirit. They are dependable, excellent followers, "rule enforcers", and absolutely loyal. They are not very strong willed, are not great at decision making, and struggle with low self-esteem.

Most people are a blend of two or more temperaments. Every temperament has strengths and weaknesses, and the Holy Spirit can work to transform the weaknesses in our temperaments. Dr. LaHaye's other book, *Transformed Temperaments*, is a biblical study of how Peter, Paul, Moses and Abraham's temperaments were transformed and used by God.

2. Core Values

Your values are the intangible preferences you feel strongly about, that drive your actions, and that you give great weight to in decision making. They are the moral codes and principles that form the guardrails of your life, and play a big role in your daily choices, priorities, persuading and influencing, communication, and conflict resolution. They are your non-negotiables, your internal score card. Compromising them would lead to great internal stress and conflict. For example, if family is a core value, then when you are faced with a conflict, you will make a choice that elevates family over other priorities. Your values help you to self-start, stay motivated, stay on course, be intentional, and make good choices. Your values are your personal code, internal framework, value system and worldview. It is how you determine right and wrong, and staying true to them helps you to maintain healthy self-respect and a good view of yourself.

3. Strengths & Weaknesses

Your strengths include your skills, talents, and abilities. This is the area where you are naturally equipped to excel. It also includes your character strengths like loyalty, integrity, respect, perseverance, and so on. Identifying your "strength zone", the core area where you have a convergence of skills, abilities and interests, is very important to success and fulfillment in life. Also, knowing your strength zone is one of the foundations of self-esteem, self-confidence, and internal security. Knowing your weaknesses is equally important. It enables you to be self-aware, realistic, and honest with yourself. Knowing your strengths and weaknesses promote confidence, humility and most of all, a balanced and healthy view of yourself.

4. Interests

To discover your interests, ask yourself the following questions. What do you like to do? What draws and holds your attention? What would you like to do for free? Interests add passion, zest and gusto to life. They provide valuable insight, not only about what you want, like or dislike, but why. It also helps to confirm your core values. Your interests can provide the road map to your future career, spouse, and so on. Working at a job that lines up with your interests will position you to succeed and give you a tremendous sense of fulfillment and wellbeing.

5. Body

Know your body constitution, shape, ability, and tolerances; what colors you like, what types of clothes look good on you, and so on. Know your biorhythms. Are you a morning person? At what time of day does your energy peak? Knowing your body helps you to maximize your potential. For example, planning activities when you are at your best ensures success, plus it respects your innate biology. "Your daily life is more pleasant when you are in sync with your biology. In every area, it is easier to enjoy life when you don't waste energy pretending to be someone you aren't." Knowing your body includes being a good steward of your body – leading a healthy lifestyle, investing in personal grooming, learning what foods work best for your body, having regular health checkups, saying no to drugs, alcohol, and sexual immorality, and incorporating regular exercise as part of your body care regimen. Your body is a limited resource. Knowing your body helps you to maximize your body's potential.

6. Dreams

Many people are embarrassed about their dreams. They feel awkward about sharing their dreams, because they think it's too farfetched, or that others would laugh at them for "day dreaming". Others hide their dreams because the realities of daily life mock their dreams. However, dreams are very important in the life of a Christian, for two reasons. First, God could be, and often is the source of your dreams. If you have a strong, innate desire or dream to do something that is in line with the word of God, it could very well be God putting that desire in your heart. The Bible states that "God is working in you, giving you the desire and power to do what pleases him" (Philippians 2:13). If you have a strong dream or desire about the future, treasure it and pray about it. God may have put that desire in your heart and He can help you fulfill it.

Secondly, your dreams give you a blueprint of the future you want, so you can partner with God to create it. In other words, your dreams provide a glimpse into your future. In my book *"Choosing a Life of Victory,* I discussed how God gave us the ability to create our world, just like He created the world. Your dreams give you the blueprint of the world, your world, that you want to create. Write down your dreams, include the details and specifics, and pray about it. The Bible says, "Write the vision; engrave it so plainly upon tablets that everyone who passes may be able to read it easily and quickly as he hastens by. This vision is for a future time. It describes the end, and it will be fulfilled. If it seems slow in coming, wait patiently, for it will surely take place. It will not be delayed" (Habakkuk 2:2-3).

Writing down your dream forces you to organize your thoughts. It helps mature your dream from wishful thinking to an executable plan. It also helps promote critical thinking about a strategy to achieve the dream. Writing your dream in detail equips you with an invaluable ability to recognize and identify opportunities and individuals who will help bring your dream to reality. Also, writing down your dream gets you invested, and allows you to deploy the power of creative thinking, perseverance, and faith to bring your dream to pass. Simply stated, writing down your dream give it life!

7. Purpose

To discover your purpose, ask yourself the following questions "What are the most meaningful events of my life? What gives me joy and deep personal satisfaction? What makes me cry? Answering these questions will help you find out how you are wired, and "You may discover clues to your hidden identity, to your career, and to life satisfaction". Also, understanding your temperament and temperament blends will help you identify your natural predisposition, and how you interact with people, places and things. Temperament is your internal wiring by God that prepares you to fulfill His purpose for your life.

Knowing your core building blocks of self allows you to love yourself in the way that God intended. It frees you to be you and not have to apologize for it. Acting on that self-knowledge is liberating! It sets you free from laboring to conform to how you, or others think you "should" feel, think, or act. It promotes an internal consistency that is so critical to self-definition. It energizes and strengthens you to interface with others as the authentic you, and to genuinely love them without being needy, clingy or codependent. It gives you a screen with which to evaluate the people in your life and determine who belongs and who doesn't. Ultimately, it gives you the freedom to rest and nest in God!

Loving Others

Now that we have examined what it means to love ourselves, Jesus's directive to us is to "love your neighbor as yourself." Jesus then told a parable to illustrate the point.

The Parable of the Good Samaritan

In Luke 10, an expert in Jewish law tested Jesus with a question. He said, "Teacher, what should I do to inherit eternal life?" Jesus told him to love God and his neighbor. The man wanted to justify his actions, so he asked Jesus, "And who is my neighbor?" Jesus replied with a story: "A Jewish man was traveling from Jerusalem down to Jericho, and he was attacked by bandits. They stripped him of his clothes, beat him up, and left him half dead beside the road. "By chance a priest came along. But when he saw the man lying there, he crossed to the other side of the road and passed him by. A Temple assistant walked over and looked at him lying there, but he also passed by on the other side. "Then a despised Samaritan came along, and when he saw the man, he felt compassion for him. Going over to him, the Samaritan soothed his wounds with olive oil and wine and bandaged them. Then he put the man on his own donkey and took him to an inn, where he took care of him. The next day he handed the innkeeper two silver coins, telling him, 'Take care of this man. If his bill runs higher than this, I'll pay you the next time I'm here.' "Now which of these three would you say was a neighbor to the man who was attacked by bandits?" Jesus asked. The man replied, "The one who showed him mercy." Then Jesus said, "Yes, now go and do the same."

In this parable, Jesus teaches the following lessons about loving others.

1. **Love Without Bias or Prejudice**: Jesus's choice of the cast for this parable was very deliberate. At the heart of this story are ancient ethnic and religious biases and prejudices. Simply stated, the Jews hated the Samaritans. Who are the Samaritans? They are the mixed multitude, the ethnic and religious outsiders. "When the Assyrians destroyed the Northern Kingdom of Israel in 722, they exiled the upper crust of society in order to deprive the country of its leadership. At the same time, as they did elsewhere, they brought in foreign elements in order to create a mixed population unlikely to unify and revolt. These new elements eventually mixed with the native population and together they evolved a syncretistic form of Israelite worship" (Schiffman). These were the Samaritans.

   To love the Jewish man who had been hurt, the Samaritan had to step over centuries old biases and prejudices. Jesus said for us to "go and do the same"; meaning, this is how we should love others, without prejudice and bias.

2. **Love Without Judgement:** To the Jews listening to this parable, it was unthinkable that the despised Samaritan would be the hero of this story. This parable teaches us that love does not judge people on the basis of their ethnicity or religious denomination. Of note, this parable was set at a time and culture when most Jews believed that if bad things happened to you, you probably deserved them, because of your sin or low living. In addition, given the Jewish religious laws and customs, if you got involved to help the injured man, you might render yourself unclean, and unfit for worship or communal life. This may have been one of the reasons why the priest and temple assistant did not want to get involved; and passed by on the other side. But the Samaritan reached out to love without judgement, and without regard to the impact on his own social status.

3. **Love Values People:** The Samaritan placed a high value on people over money, reputation, time, prejudices, religious observances, other people's opinion, and his own convenience. He loved like God! God greatly values people, and He wants us to value people too. Our love must be an expression of the value we place on others as bearing the imprint and image of God.

4. **Love Your Enemies:** Jews and Samaritans were arch enemies. The injured Jew could have been a "Samaritan-hater", and may even have personally despised and mistreated Samaritans in the past. But that is irrelevant. God does not hold us accountable for the actions or prejudices of

others, but for our own. Regardless of what the injured Jew in particular, or Jews in general, may have done to this particular Samaritan, or Samaritans generally in the past, God's love requires us to love anyway. In Matthew 5:44, Jesus said, "Love your enemies, bless those who hate you, and pray for those who persecute you".

5. **Love Compassionately**: This parable teaches us that loving others means acting in their best interest. Compassion is love in action. It means that when you see a need, you should own it and do what you can to solve it. The Samaritan did not need to hear a sermon or for God to "speak" to him to help. He saw a need, was moved with compassion, and acted to address the need. This is the pattern that Jesus laid out in the scriptures. Several scriptures record that Jesus saw a need, was "moved with compassion" and took action to meet the need. For example, Matthew 9:36, Luke 7:12-15. We should do likewise.

6. **Love Sacrificially:** Loving others has a cost. In this parable, it cost the Samaritan money, time, attention, his own convenience, and so on. He went out of his way to care for the wounded man. He put the man on his donkey. The Jew rode and the Samaritan walked. Sometimes, loving others will take us outside our comfort zone, or cause us significant inconvenience, like it did the Samaritan.

7. **Get Others Involved to Help**: The Samaritan did all he could do, but he did not stop there. He enlisted the inn keeper to help. Sometimes, we are not in a position to help

or are poorly equipped, or what we can do is limited, but we can invite and encourage others to help. The principle is, do what you can and invite others to join in.

8. **Follow Up:** The Samaritan cared enough not only to help in the moment, but to follow up later. He went over and beyond. Sometimes we are tempted to do the least we can, or to put up an appearance, or go through the motions of helping. But 1 John 3:18 challenges us to "love not in word and speech, but with actions and in truth."

Whole people are people who love and value themselves and others in the name of the Lord. Love personifies God, so, there is no wholeness without love.

Love Languages

Just like people communicate verbally with words to be understood, love has a language. And just like speaking the English language to a person who understands only the Chinese Mandarin language will make for a very frustrating, unintelligible and bizarre "conversation", speaking love to a person in a love language that they do not understand has the exact same effect. It is gibberish. So, for two people to effectively communicate love, it is important to find out the love language that the other person speaks, learn that language and use it to communicate your love to them.

There are 5 love languages. These were popularized in the 1992 book, *The Five Love Languages,* by Gary Chapman. Each person has a primary love language which speaks more to them than all the others. Discovering that language and speaking it regularly is the best way to say "I love you" to that individual.

1. **Words of Affirmation:** This love language entails using words to build up the other person. They could be words of appreciation for specific actions, qualities or accomplishments; or expressions of personal value, worth, affirmation and validation. These expressions can be communicated verbally or written in a card, love note, email, text and so on.

2. **Gifts**: This love language entails giving a gift. To the recipient, the gift says, "I value you" or "I was thinking about you". It also says, "you are so important to me that I took time out of my day to find this gift for you".

3. **Acts of Service**: This love language involves doing something for the other person that you know they would appreciate. It could range from getting them a cup of water, running bath water, giving them a massage, or helping around the house. It is important that you learn what the other person likes, and not merely give them what you like or think they should like.

4. **Quality Time**: For individuals with this love language, love is spelt TIME. This involves spending time with the other person and giving them your undivided attention. Note that it is not just being there physically, while your mind is miles away. You need to be fully present, engaged, making

eye contact, nodding, reflecting what you hear, actively listening and responding.

5. **Physical Touch**: This is love that is expressed through tactile contact – holding hands, touching, playful pinching, patting, massage, hugging, kissing and so on. Guys, if this is your wife's love language, it is important that you speak this language to her without a hidden agenda, and not as a prelude to sex.

Sexuality and the Christian

God created sex, sexuality and sexual desire in men and women. Psalms 139:14 states that we are fearfully and wonderfully made. However, the Bible is clear that God ordained for sex to be practiced within the confines of marriage. Contrary to the lies told by Hollywood, "Genuine love and relationship outside of marriage does not require sexual expression for fulfillment". Sex outside of marriage is a contravention of God's standards and can be very destructive. For a married person, sex outside of marriage is adultery, and for a single person, it is fornication. In the Bible, adultery and fornication are collectively referred to as sexual immorality.

God has very strong words against sexual immorality. In 1 Corinthians 6:18, the Bible says, "Run from sexual sin! No other sin so clearly affects the body as this one does. For sexual immorality is a sin against your own body". This scripture states categorically that sexual sin is unlike any other sin. It is in a class all by itself, because when you engage in sexual immorality, you not only sin against the Lord, and other people, but you also sin against your own body.

Sexual Immorality is a Grave Sin Against the Lord

1. **Your Body Is A Temple That Houses the Holy Spirit.** First Corinthians 6:19 states, "Don't you realize that your body is the temple of the Holy Spirit, who lives in you and was given to you by God?". The Holy Spirit lives in you, so, every time you engage in sexual immorality, you are dragging the Holy Spirit, kicking and screaming and forcing Him to lay down and engage in that sexual encounter with you. You are forcing Him to fornicate or commit adultery! You are forcing Him to have sex against His will. You are raping the Holy Spirit!

2. **God's Temple Is Holy, Sexual Sin Defiles and Destroys This Temple.** First Corinthians 3:16-17 states, "Don't you realize that you are the temple of God and that the Spirit of God lives in you? God will destroy anyone who destroys this temple. For God's temple is holy, and you are that temple". When you engage in sexual sin, you set yourself on a collision course with destruction. Why? Because sexual sin destroys your body. Your body is God's holy temple, and when you defile and destroy God's temple, God Himself will destroy anyone (including you), who destroys His temple.

3. **You Belong to God.** First Corinthians 7:20 states, "You do not belong to yourself, for God bought you with a high price. So you must honor God with your body." And Romans 12:1-2, instructs us to give our bodies to God and, "Let them be a living

and holy sacrifice—the kind he will find acceptable. This is truly the way to worship him". In other words, sexual purity and abstinence honors God and is a living and holy sacrifice of true worship.

4. **God is Holy**. First Peter 1:14-16 states, "So you must live as God's obedient children. Don't slip back into your old ways of living to satisfy your own desires. You didn't know any better then. But now you must be holy in everything you do, just as God who chose you is holy. For the Scriptures say, "You must be holy because I am holy." This scripture quotes Leviticus 11:44. "The word translated "holy" means sacred, morally blameless, consecrated, saint". Habakkuk 1:13 puts it in context. It says of God, "Your eyes are too pure to look on evil and you cannot tolerate wrongdoing". This is why Jesus felt the desolate separation from His father when He was carrying our sins on the cross. God's eyes are too pure to look on evil. So, He turned His face away from His Son, when He hung on the cross gruesomely disfigured by the sins of mankind. Can you then imagine the unspeakable horror and utter despicableness of forcing God, who lives in your body, to be an accomplice to and a participant in sexual sin?

Why Are Sexual Sins Worse Than Other Sins?

Pastor Jack Hayford wrote an excellent book on this subject, titled "*Fatal Attractions*". In it, he details several reasons why sexual sins are worse than other sins, and especially destructive to the individual engaged in it. Following are some excerpts from that book.

1. Sex Sins Stain the Root of An Individual's Identity

This is the first and foundational reason why sex sins are worse than any other sin. "In the raw physiological facts of life, there is nothing so fundamental to our personhood as our genitals..... the first way in which any of us was identified was either "it's a boy" or "it's a girl"—a fact that is far more deeply related to our whole sense of who we are than most of us are willing to acknowledge." This is why there is such a "deep sense of loss and isolation that occurs when the foundation of a person's identity is violated by sexual pollution." When we first brush up against sexual immorality, it evokes something deep within us. "Notice is served from the first—before our consciences are seared through by recurrent acts—that the root of our identities has been touched in an inappropriate way, and we begin to feel a sense of loss—a shattering, a straining—as the very foundation of who we are has been shaken and violated" "An entire lifetime can be crippled, and a hopeful future can progressively disintegrate when one's identity is polluted by sexual sin".

2. Sex Sins Exploit the Deepest Aspects of Our Emotionality

"Because sexual activity awakens our deepest passions, it also exposes us to the greatest risk of emotional violation and injury". "Since nothing is more emotionally or physically provocative than our sexuality...Sexual indulgence is deceitfully presented as a means to physically prove a person's worth (or prowess), emotionally violating those who are desperate to sense they deeply matter to other people and who yearn to feel loved."

We live in a time when sexual immorality is portrayed as the norm, infidelity is romanticized in popular music, blatant lust is falsely paraded as love, and sexual compromise is widespread. So many emotionally vulnerable women are exploited by men who disguise their warped and self-centered sexual demands as love. "If you love me, you'll do this" they say, but the woman finds out, too late, that the promised love and emotional support was all a farce. "Contrary to the bill of goods that's been sold to society, breaking every sexual convention and taboo hasn't brought any of us more liberty, only more enslavement and brokenness." Individuals who are secure in their true identity in Christ will not feel a need to prove themselves through their sexual prowess or "by allowing their personhood, values and body to be violated".

3. Sexual Sins Pollute the Fountainhead of Our Highest Creativity

"Sin of all kinds---but particularly sex sins---poison us at the root of our identity, humanity and creativity." God created us in His own image, with the ultimate ability, the ability to create life, eternal life, at will. This is the God-kind ability that separates mankind from all other creation. And this is the ability that is vandalized, abused, distorted and corrupted by sexual sin. Jesus said that the devil comes to "steal, kill and destroy". In no other area of life is this tri-fold satanic ministry more manifest and prolific than in the sexual area. When sexual immorality is given full rein, it consumes a person's time, thought and resources. The mind, creative faculties and daily activities are preoccupied with how to find or create more opportunities for sex. This blind focus deadens the spirit, dominates the mental capacity, snuffs out any creativity and consumes all available resources. The thief is at work! These "little burglaries that we let Satan get away with … lead to the wholesale robbery of all that matters to us." "God desires that we would see the meeting point between our spiritual and our physical capacities. If we do not learn the *discipline* of His ways in our sexual capacities (which are a part of His creative design in us), then we will never learn the *glory* of His creative capacity working through us in a spiritual dimension".

4. Sex Sins Produce Guilt That Cripples Confidence and Authority

"More than any other kind of sin, sexual sin produces guilt that cripples a believer's confidence and authority." "This sense of guilt and shame does not persist because the individuals do not understand God's forgiveness; it persists because of two dynamics: first, the brutality of the adversary, and second, the vulnerability of our sexuality to unique psychological wounding." "When people surrender to sexual sin, it is common for something real to become lodged in their souls—something fixes itself in the psyche, like a monument to their failure". They feel a crushing sense of guilt and condemnation even though they have a personal relationship with Christ, know about His love, mercy, and forgiveness; and that the Bible says that they are forgiven. They still feel the unshakeable, debilitating imprint of guilt, shame, reproach and condemnation. Sexual sin has left an invisible brand on their soul.

5. **Sex Sins Increase the Probability of Multiplying the Spread of Disease**

"The crippling shame and emotional damage of sex sins leave a permanent mark on the psyche—and often a fatal mark in the flesh of a person who has contracted a sexually transmitted disease". HIV, herpes, gonorrhea, and many other sexually transmitted diseases have ruined lives, and destroyed their victim's hopes for having children. Nothing in life is as bitter as the regret and self-loathing of a person who knows that they are unable to marry, conceive, or raise the family that they always wanted, because of their prior sexual indiscretions. Part of the heavy weight of their self-blame come from knowing that their actions have also negatively impacted their spouse for a lifetime. Unfortunately, people are deluded into a false sense of security, either because they think that they practice "safe sex", or because they believe that there are medications available for these infections. Even though available medications may cure some of these diseases, the scar tissue or other residual issue that they leave behind often have a long term impact on the ability to conceive or raise a family.

6. **Sex Sins Give Place to Appetites That Only Beget Further Immoral Behavior**

When a person engages in sexual sin, like fornication, adultery, or watching pornography, a spiritual transaction takes place and he or she is corrupted by a demon of lust. This demon makes you feel justified in giving yourself the license for sexual gratification. You feel that you "deserve" sex and sexual pleasure. This sense of entitlement blurs your spiritual perception and short circuits good judgement. Essentially, your brain is now between your legs. "God's word speaks so strongly because licentiousness bypasses God's monitors on the human heart that help to establish our values…..And once given license, the spirit of lust begins its deceptive seduction". Eventually, the individual will go far beyond the bounds of what is "normal". They will develop extreme sexual appetites that "normal" sex will no longer be sufficient. Consequently, they progressively engage in more and more risky or extreme sexual behavior, looking for a "high". Often, they turn to drugs to heighten their sexual pleasure and this leads to even more bondage. "Women who dabble in sexual flirtation or use sex as a means to obtain emotional or material favors from men find themselves equally surrendered to the spirit of lust, in bondage and struggling for control". A collateral damage of this depraved, demonic, appetite for sex is the current or future spouse, who despite their best efforts, will never be able to satisfy this individual. This is why marriage does not solve this problem. The individual needs deliverance from the spirit of lust.

I highly recommend Pastor Hayford's book, *Fatal Attractions*. It covers several other reasons why sexual sins are worse than other sins and provides real life stories from Pastor Jack's counseling ministry.

Soul Ties and Spiritual Orbits

A soul tie is a strong connection or bond that binds two people in the soul realm. Their two souls are "knit" together in an intense bond, such that they "cleave" to each other and become "one flesh".

One of the primary ways that a soul tie is created is through sexual intimacy. God intended sex for marriage, so He included in the plan, a godly soul tie to be established during sex. This strong bond or connection draws a married couple together like magnets, they feel a special closeness, belonging, yearning, completeness and oneness with each other. Their two souls are melded together and they feel inseparable. Ephesians 5:31 describes this process, "For this cause shall a man leave his father and mother, and shall be joined to his wife and they two shall become one flesh". This soul tie creates a bridge between their two souls. Over time, they can know each other very deeply, communicate very effectively without using words, finish each other's sentences, and become essentially an extension of each other. This is why the biblical expression for sex is "to know". The first biblical record of sex is in Genesis 4:1, "And the man knew Eve his wife; and she conceived". This deep, intimate "knowing" establishes a soul tie.

A soul tie can also be formed between close friends. First Samuel 18:1 provides an example of a good soul tie between David and Jonathan. "Now when he had finished speaking to Saul, the soul of Jonathan was knit to the soul of David, and Jonathan loved him as his own soul."

Having a soul tie allows a married couple to be in each other's spiritual orbit. As we studied earlier, every person is a spirit, has a soul and lives in a body. Each person's soul has its own orbit, like a planet. People who are in, share, or intersect with our orbits are people we care deeply about or are in committed, long term, covenant relationships with, such as family members, close friends and relatives. When people are in your orbit, they have access to your soul realm, and can "sense" when something is going on with you. They tend to call "just at the right time" or you were just thinking about them, and they show up or you run into them, and so on. For a married couple, family members and close godly friends, being in each other's orbit is a blessing. They can accurately "sense" things about the other person, or "feel" a need to pray for them, or simply "know" that something is wrong, even when they are thousands of miles apart. This helps them to support and cover one another.

When a person has sex outside of marriage, an ungodly soul tie is formed. First Corinthians 6:16 describes this process, "And don't you realize that if a man joins himself to a prostitute, he becomes one body with her? For the Scriptures say, "The two are united into one." If they have sex outside of marriage with multiple people, this further complicates the issue, leads to tremendous fragmentation in the soul realm, and this person will have a difficult time bonding with a spouse, because they are still connected to these other people. Also, because soul ties create a bridge between two souls, sex outside of marriage opens up demonic traffic between the two people such that there can be a transference of evil spirits, demonic strongholds, satanic bonds, generational curses, ancestral spirits, oppressive covenants, emotional torment, and so on. For example, if a person has sex with another person who has the demon of lust, that unclean spirit can latch on to this other person, gain access into their lives and they too will begin to go down the path of sexual excess. If the person that they slept with has had multiple sexual partners, that also opens them up to contracting all the spiritual, emotional and physical corruption, and pollution from all those other partners.

In addition, personal vows and other affirmations of love and commitment that people make to each other during sex or the course of an affair or other sexually involved relationship can also create a soul tie. Often in the heat of lustful passion, a couple can say to each other, "I can never feel this way about another woman or man", "I could never love another man/woman" "I will love you forever", and so on. These types of verbal commitments and covenants are essentially like marriage vows. They are intended for committed marital relationships, but when they are made within the context of sex outside of marriage, they confuse and bind the soul. When the relationship breaks up and the parties part ways, they have to go through an emotional pain and trauma that is very much like a divorce, even though they were not married.

Soul ties are the reasons why many abused women make excuses for and keep going back to the same man who had physically, verbally and sexually abused them, doesn't love them and treats them like dirt. It is also the reason why a guy who breaks up with a woman and doesn't want her, all of a sudden gets insanely jealous and territorial over her when she starts going out with another man. Murders without number have been committed because of soul ties.

Also, when you have sex outside of marriage, you open up the door and let your sexual partner into your spiritual orbit. This is because the sex act involves a very deep level of "knowing", soul interlocking, physical intimacy, vulnerability and connection. Same thing can happen when you have close friends and confidants who are not believers in Christ. These deep connections where you "bare your soul" to another person can establish a strong bond in the soul realm. Have you ever wondered why when you finally make up your mind to become serious with God and grow in your relationship with Him, you "just happen" to get a call from your former unsaved boyfriend? Or why, when you are in a vulnerable state emotionally, you just happen to "run into" that girl or guy that you slept with years ago and s/he talks you into having sex again? Or why you just happen to meet a person "by chance" who becomes a big negative influence in your life for evil? Or why you keep feeling this strong gravitational pull to a person, place or activity that you know is toxic for you? It's a set up by the devil. He will try to tell you that these incidents are "a sign" that "it was meant to be" or that you are supposed to be with these people, but that is a lie. The truth is that you opened yourself up, through unholy connections, and granted access to the wrong people, so that your orbit attracts or intersects with these people who are agents of the devil, with an assignment from hell to destroy your life.

Sexual Images

A powerful token of sexual sin, and the soul ties that it engenders, are the associated images. Sexual sin generates passionate images that linger and evoke strong emotions. Whether they are images from actual sexual encounters, or pornographic images, these images appear to be branded in the mind, and become strong chains that bind and hold the individual captive. Often, even after the individual has decided to walk away from the sin of sexual immorality, they cannot get rid of the images, and at the opportune moment, the devil energizes those images, empowers them, and use them to bring the person down. These attacks are especially vicious, intense and swift. A person who has repented from sexual sin, can have sudden, overpowering, flashback images of sexual acts with a person that they felt especially close to, or had a "special" connection with, or had a sexual relationship with over a long period of time. These attacks are swift and effective; the image is suddenly introduced into the mind, backed by very strong emotions, and before you know it, it hijacks the thought process, and moves your will to commit a sexual sin. The pressure is intense, and these images become the access points, or tokens for the demon of lust to reenter, retake possession, and take the person down. These attacks leave the individual feeling powerless and defeated. The shame, repeated failure, and feeling of helplessness to break free, drive the individual to depression, hopelessness, and despair. Many feel trapped, and some consider suicide.

How to Break Soul Ties

1. **Stop:** Stop crying to God to save you. He already has done His part; the next move is yours. You made wrong choices that led you into sexual bondage. You can make different choices to take you out, starting now.

2. **Repent**: Confess the sexual sin(s) and genuinely repent before God.

3. **Forgive:** Forgive the other person if you have any lingering issues or offense.

4. **Destroy Any Tokens:** Any tokens such as gifts, rings, flowers, love letters, photos, and so on, given or received in connection with the sexual relationship should be destroyed.

5. **Uproot Root of Bitterness:** In Hebrews 12:15, the Bible points out that a root of bitterness will bring corruption and immorality into your life. Uproot any bitterness in your heart, and lay it before the Lord.

6. **Cancel Every Vow:** Any personal vows or verbal commitments that supported or helped form the soul tie should be renounced and revoked. Since they were enacted verbally, you can undo and cancel them verbally.

9. **Renounce and Revoke the Soul Tie:** Declare, "In Jesus name, I renounce and revoke every soul tie formed between me and _____ as a result of our sexual sin. Jesus has forgiven me and set me free. I declare my freedom in Christ.

10. **Break the Soul Tie:** Exercise your authority in Christ to sever the soul tie. Declare, "In Jesus name, I now break, dismantle and sever any ungodly soul ties formed between me and_____. I declare it to be null, void and of no effect. Jesus has set me free, and whom the Son sets free is free indeed. I declare and walk in my freedom in Christ.

11. **Cast Down the Images:** Second Corinthians 10:4 states that we have power, through God to cast down imaginations. If these images arise in your head, speak up and rebuke them in the name of Jesus. Dismantle and cast them down. Do not allow them to complete. Declare that your imagination is flooded with the light of God (Ephesians 1:18).

12. **Appropriate the Blood of Jesus:** Declare that the blood of Jesus purchased your salvation and deliverance. All your sins, including your sexual sins were paid in full. There is no condemnation for those who are in Christ, so you reject every voice that speaks against you in judgement and condemnation. Declare that the blood of Jesus is speaking over you, freedom, deliverance, victory, strength, and grace.

13. **Stay Full of God's Word:** Fill your mind with God's word, and you will have no room for Satan's lies and snares.

How Can I Be Sexually Pure?

When Jesus redeemed the woman caught in adultery, He said to her, "go and sin no more" (John 8:10-11). It is of critical importance that after breaking, and being delivered from a soul tie, that you maintain sexual purity. Jesus warns us that when an unclean spirit is cast out of a person, it goes around, looking for an alternate place to reside, and finding none, it will come back to the "house" or person from whom it was cast out, and if their soul space is clean but empty, the evil spirit would go and recruit seven other spirits more evil than himself, and they will re-occupy that life, and the person is worse off than before they were delivered (Luke 11:24-26,

Matthew 12:43-45). This is why it is crucial to maintain sexual purity going forward. Here's how:

1. **Believe That Sexual Purity is Possible and You Have the Power:** To be sexually pure, you must believe that sexual purity is possible, and that you are well able, through Christ, to live a pure life. Despite the lies that the depraved culture, media, and the devil is propagating, not "everybody is doing it". On the contrary, there is an army of single Christian men and women who are living a genuinely celibate lifestyle that honors the Lord. I am one of them. To the glory of God, I have been celibate for over 10 years, and pure in mind and body. It is one of the most powerful testimonies of my life, to be able to look my children in the eye, and affirm to them, that I have honored the Lord in my sexuality. You can too! All you need to do, is to make different choices. Following are the principles that have helped me and countless others to live sexually pure in a corrupt and polluted world. These principles will work for you, if you, with the help of the Holy Spirit, apply them to your life.

2. **The First Place to Start Is in the Mind**: Sexual purity begins with your thoughts. You must set aside what you think about sex outside of marriage and agree with God that it is a terrible sin. You must see, think, believe and feel about it, the way God does. Sex outside of marriage is not okay, it is not exciting, it is not the cultural norm, it is not fun, it is not a mistake, it is a sin and an egregious breach against a Holy and righteous God.

3. **You Must See Your Body as Physically a Part of Christ**: This makes your engagement in sexual sin a gross violation of the Lord himself. It makes it tantamount to raping Christ. The Bible says, "Don't you realize that your bodies are actually parts of Christ? Should a man take his body, which is part of Christ, and join it to a prostitute?" The emphatic answer comes back, "Never!" (1 Corinthians 6:15). That should be your feelings exactly! Whenever confronted with the choice to engage in sexual sin, your response should always be an emphatic, "Never".

4. **Don't Excuse or Justify Sexual Sin:** Tear down the wrong reasoning, thought process and self-talk that justifies and excuses the sin of sexual immorality. This is the thought process that says, "I can do anything I want. I am not hurting anybody." First Corinthians 6:12 confronts this argument head on and exposes the lie. It states, "You say, "I am allowed to do anything"—but not everything is good for you. And even though "I am allowed to do anything," I must not become a slave to anything." Nothing is so "not good for you" and enslaves so quickly and completely as sexual sin. The crushing feelings of guilt, condemnation, worthlessness, personal loathing, erosion of the sense of self, personal dignity and value that follow is massive and debilitating. Not to mention the waves of emptiness and craving that drives the person back again and again for more, until they are on the brink of hopelessness and despair.

As overseer of the prayer ministries at our church, I have counseled so many people trapped in sexual sin. The story and the resulting devastation is usually the same. Sexual sin promises excitement and fulfillment, but it ends up leaving people in a dark, deep pit, ashamed, estranged from God, hating themselves, and sorely afraid. The behavior that once provided illicit pleasure now leaves them scarred, and branded with an invisible brand on their soul.

At church, I also served in a ministry that called first time guests who visited our church and requested prayer. I will never forget one woman that I called. As soon as I identified who I was, she began to weep; deep, heaving sobs. I held the phone, waited and prayed. I thought she had just lost a family member. Eventually she quieted down enough to tell me what happened. She was a single Christian woman who had been living for God. That day, she gave in to temptation and had sex. She was an absolute wreck! That sin violated and wounded her so deeply. Whatever temporary pleasure she had experienced was totally eclipsed by the torrent of shame, guilt and brokenness she felt. I think back to that woman often. For her, and so many others whom I have counseled, it was not worth it, not in the least.

5. **You Must Tear Down the Wrong Reasoning**: Tear down the thought process and self-talk that justifies sexual sin as fulfilling a legitimate need. This is the lie that says, sex is a natural need just like food. I need sex, just like I need food. God made me a sexual being, so my craving for sex outside of marriage is a legitimate natural need, and so, I can and should satisfy my sexual cravings. First Corinthians 6:13-14 addresses and challenges this lie. "You say, "Food was made for the stomach, and the stomach for food." But you can't say that our bodies were made for sexual immorality. They were made for the Lord, and the Lord cares about our bodies." God made both our stomachs and our sexual parts. And here the

Bible states emphatically that the comparison is false. Yes, food was made for the stomach and the stomach for food, but our bodies were not made for sexual immorality. Our bodies were made for the Lord, and sex outside of marriage violates that purpose, pollutes our soul, and corrupts and destroys the body. God created our bodies and He created sex. He has told us plainly that the only proper exercise of our sexual appetites is within marriage.

6. **Make a Personal Commitment to Sexual Purity**: Dedicate your sexual parts to God as instruments of righteousness and ask Him for grace and help to live sexually pure. Romans 6:12-13 states, "Do not let sin control the way you live; do not give in to sinful desires. Do not let any part of your body become an instrument of evil to serve sin. Neither present your body parts to sin as instruments of unrighteousness; but present yourselves to God, as alive from the dead and your body parts as instruments of righteousness unto God" This scripture directs us to be intentional and to take decisive action to dedicate our sexuality and sexual parts completely to God, to honor and glorify Him. This is exactly what Joseph did. He had made a commitment to God to be sexually pure. So, when Potiphar's wife accosted and tried to seduce him, his mind was already made up and his response was clear, "How could I do such a wicked thing? It would be a great sin against God" (Genesis 39:9). The lesson is clear. Decide now what your convictions are about sexual sin, and determine in advance what your response will be when tempted to engage in sexual immorality. If you wait until you are facing temptation, to begin to debate in your mind what you should do, it will be too late, you will be overtaken.

7. **Guard the Gateways to Your Mind and Your Imagination**: Guard your eye gate, your ear gate and your mouth gate. Shut the door on anything that pollutes your mind sexually. Jesus taught that no one commits sexual sin physically who has not already done so mentally and emotionally (Matthew 5:28). So, the place to stop sexual immorality, is to stop it from dominating the thoughts and growing into lust. James 1:14-15 describes the progression: "Temptation comes from our own desires, which entice us and drag us away. These desires give birth to sinful actions. And when sin is allowed to grow, it gives birth to death".

What this means practically, is that you guard what you expose yourself to through the television, music, radio, magazines, and so on. Take authority over your eyes! You simply cannot feed your mind sexually explicit material when you are seeking to live pure. When the movie "Wolf of Wall Street" came out, I went to see it. Unfortunately, I had relied on someone else's recommendation and did not do my own research. I was told that it was a good movie, so I decided to go and see it. Well, I had to get up and walk out during the movie, due to the sexually explicit material. I could not sit there and consume that filth and expect my mind to be sexually pure. Why torture yourself? Why expose yourself to impure material and then struggle to stay pure? I understand that there is so much sexual content everywhere and it is hard to find clean material. However, a firm commitment to sexual purity requires that you invest the time and resources to identify leisure activities, and viewing material that is clean. For me, what that means is that for relaxation, when I am not watching the Christian channels, I watch old movies, westerns, and sitcoms. I find that even though they are not "Christian", they were produced at a time when "wholesome family values" coincided more with Judeo Christian values, and so they tend to have moral themes and outcomes, and little, if any, sexual content. For more modern clean movies, I sometimes watch the Hallmark channels. Also, there are many Christian movies available through Christian TV channels or online. One note of caution. A negative side effect of watching old sitcoms and westerns, is that they tend to be overloaded with commercials advertising medicines for the elderly. I mute or skip them, so I don't have that junk lodged in my mind either.

8. **Fill Your Mind and Heart with the Word of God:** If you fill your mind with the word of God, then there is no room for impure thoughts and images. Daily study and ongoing meditation on the word of God, talking to God throughout the day, regular church attendance, listening to Christian programming on TV, playing worship music, and serving others, will saturate your mind with the Word. Psalm 119:9 puts it succinctly, "How can a young person stay pure? By obeying your word." This applies equally to older people as well. Psalm 119:11 echoes the same theme, "I have hidden your word in my heart that I might not sin against you." And 1 Thessalonians 4:3 makes it crystal clear that our sexual purity is God's will. So many Christians ask, "what is God's will for my life?" Well, here it is, in black and white. "For this is the will of God, your sanctification, that you abstain from sexual immorality". It doesn't get clearer than this.

9. **Identify Your Triggers:** At the beginning of this chapter, we discussed the critical import of self-knowledge, and how knowing

yourself can help you identify your personal triggers – your appetites, proclivities, weaknesses, and what sets you up or off. Every individual has triggers. These are internal thresholds, barriers or mechanisms that when breached or compromised, can precipitate a wrongful choice. Knowing these triggers and guarding against them is a critical piece of your armor in winning the battle against sexual immorality. Emotional vulnerability can set you up for moral failure. Also, "unmet physical needs can predispose a person to thinking thoughts, speaking words and making choices that open the door to the devil". In my book, *Choosing a Life of Victory,* I discussed four states of mind that predispose people to make poor choices. This is memorialized in the acronym HALT, which stands for hungry, angry, lonely, and tired. Do not allow yourself to get too hungry, angry, lonely, and tired. Resolve these situations quickly, and before making any foolish choices. If your trigger is a magazine, a place, a song, and so on, make a personal commitment, and work with your accountability partner to develop mechanisms to guard against your exposure to these triggers. If you watch porn on the internet, then installing electronic barriers, passcodes that you don't have access to, or software that alerts your friends and family if you wander into danger territory, can provide needed protection. Knowing your personal triggers is great, but your freedom comes when you take personal responsibility to act, based upon that knowledge.

10. **Pray and Proclaim Your Identity in Christ:** Your most potent protection against the lure and chain of sexual sin, is knowing who you are in Christ, believing what God says about you, and declaring your identity in Christ. Seeing yourself as the

righteousness of God will keep you from wallowing in the slime pit of sexual sin. Knowing that you have the mind of Christ, and are a partaker of His divine nature, empowers you to act in keeping with the truth of who you are. To illustrate, a sheep may fall into the mire, but it knows that it does not belong there and would get out as quickly as possible, shake the mud off, and trot off as fast as it can. But a pig is a different story, it will wallow in the mud and mire, because that is its natural habitat. This is why the devil works so hard to convince people trapped in sexual sin that it is not only what they do, but that it is who they are, because if they can believe that they are filthy pigs, then they will quit trying to get out and lay down in the mud. Knowing and declaring who you are in Christ empowers you to say NO to sexual temptation. Knowing that sin no longer has dominion over you, enables you to exercise your authority as a son or daughter of God and live free. Praying in that authority and power shuts down the devil's operation in your life, and terminates the destructive assignment of sexual sin.

11. **You Are Not Powerless:** This is the biggest lie of the devil, and his ultimate theft, the theft of your authority in Christ. When a person is trapped in sexual addiction, the devil's supreme tactic is to intimidate them into submission. His approach is to convince them that the odds are so much against them, that they don't even try to engage the enemy. They stop fighting and give up hope. But the devil is a liar! The truth of God is that you are not powerless against the enemy and his wiles. Nor are you powerless against the bullying and overpowering pressure of your flesh. There is power, in the name of Jesus to break every yoke. That moment that feels so hopeless, when you have fallen again into sexual sin, for what

seems like the millionth time after you've promised yourself, and God, that you will never do it again, that moment, is often when you are closest to your breakthrough. The devil is desperately trying to convince you to give up, because he knows that your deliverer, the Lord of Hosts is mighty in battle and has vanquished him. Do not give up! Stand still and see the salvation of the Lord, for the addiction you see today, you shall see it again, no more, forever, for the Lord will fight for you" (Exodus 14:14).

It is important to note that the struggle itself, is not failure, rather, it is evidence of the power of the Holy Spirit working inside you to set you free. As long as you keep crawling back up, and speaking the word of God regardless of how defeated, weary and worn you feel, you will break free from sexual bondage.

Social Media and the Quest for Love

We live in a social media world; a world that has heightened, exploited and exposed our vulnerabilities. One major area of vulnerability that has been elevated and paraded by social media, is the hunger for love, acceptance, approval, and identity. God created us with a fundamental need for love, friendship, companionship, and intimacy. However, God intended for this need to be filled through healthy relationships with our family, friends, spouse, and so on; and not by a horde of internet "friends"; who really don't know, and don't care about us. Today, people measure their worth by how many likes they get on social media, and who is following them. Individuals who have no meaningful contribution to society, have become social media "personalities", "influencers" and "celebrities." Social media has spawned a selfie generation, people who are obsessed with themselves, and love to put themselves on display. This has had tragic consequences! Vulnerable young people, looking for acceptance and love, have been crushed, publicly humiliated, and driven to suicide by vicious, public attacks and ridicule on social media.

> *We are not defined by the likes of many, but by the love of one, Jesus.*

In Genesis 29, the Bible tells the story of one woman's desperate search for love and acceptance. This is the story of Leah. Jacob did not love Leah, and was tricked into marrying her. Leah felt unwanted and unloved. She expressed her desperate search for her husband's love in the names she gave her children. She named her first born son Reuben, for she said, "The Lord has noticed my misery, and now my husband will love me". When she had her second son, she named him Simeon, for she said, "The Lord has heard that I was unloved ad has given me another son". Then she had a third son, and named him Levi, for she said "Surely this time my husband will feel affection for me, since I have given him three sons!" Her desperate longing, and yearning for her husband's affection yielded no fruit. She was as unloved, and unaccepted as ever. What a personal tragedy! Finally, she learned the lesson, that her validation, acceptance, and identity come, not from her performance, or the love of any human being, but from God alone. When she had a fourth son, she named him Judah, which means praise, for she said, "Now I will praise the Lord".

Only when she looked to the Lord, did she find the love and acceptance she so desperately needed. The Bible stated that after Judah, she stopped having children. Her soul found its rest in God.

It is little wonder that Judah became the kingly tribe in Israel, the tribe that brought forth our Lord Jesus Christ.

This is instructive for us. The Bible makes clear that our identity is not in our social media status, the number of likes or follows we have, or the love and approval of people. Our identity is in Christ alone, and only when we look to Him for love, affirmation, value, and validation, will we be made whole. Simply stated, we are not defined by the likes of many, but by the love of one, Jesus.

Unequally Yoked

A yoke is a wooden beam normally used between a pair of oxen or other animals in order to make them pull together on a load when working in pairs. It is a device, usually consisting of a crosspiece with two bow shaped pieces, each enclosing the head of the animal. The yoke enables the animals to walk close together when they are pulling a plow. "Equally yoked" means that oxen of comparable strength, height and capacity are teamed together, so that they can accomplish their task quickly and effectively. When two oxen are not "equally yoked", meaning that one is stronger than the other, or that one is taller than the other, the weaker or shorter ox would walk slower than the taller, stronger one, causing the load to go around in circles. "When oxen are unequally yoked, they cannot perform the task set before them. Instead of working together, they work at odds with one another"

Second Corinthians 6:14-18 states:

> Don't team up with those who are unbelievers. How can righteousness be a partner with wickedness? How can light live with darkness? What harmony can there be between Christ and the devil? How can a believer be a partner with an unbeliever? And what union can there be between God's temple and idols? For we are the temple of the living God. As God said: "I will live in them and walk among them. I will be their God, and they will be my people. Therefore, come out from among unbelievers, and separate yourselves from them, says the LORD. Don't touch their filthy things, and I will welcome you. And I will be your Father, and you will be my sons and daughters, says the LORD Almighty.

This scripture applies to marriage and other partnerships with a non-believer. Can you see the stark contrast that God makes?

Believer	**Unbeliever**
Righteousness	Wickedness
Light	Darkness
Christ	The devil
God's temple	Idols
Sons & daughters of God	Filthy things

The word of God is clear! A believer should not team up with, partner, live or be in business with a non-believer. God's express direction is to come out from among them and separate yourself.

This does not mean that you don't associate, work, or collaborate with an unbeliever. Jesus was often vilified for doing exactly that. What it does mean is that you don't get into a close bond, business partnership and certainly not marriage, with an unbeliever.

Unequally yoked can also mean that the two oxen are bearing altogether different yokes. For a yoke to work, both animals must submit to it and their heads must be encased in it. The device is intended to enable the animals to walk together side by side to accomplish their assignment. If one animal is wearing one yoke and the other is wearing another and completely different yoke, then they are not yoked together at all. They have nothing that binds them together. To an onlooker, they may appear to walk side by side, but that is until one decides to take off and go in a different direction, and there is no yoke to restrain it. Very importantly, two animals wearing two different yokes cannot pull the same plow. They will produce vastly different and discordant results.

In Matthew 11:28-30, Jesus said: "Come to me, all of you who are weary and carry heavy burdens, and I will give you rest. Take my yoke upon you. Let me teach you, because I am humble and gentle at heart, and you will find rest for your souls. For my yoke is easy to bear, and the burden I give you is light"

In this passage, Jesus informs us about His yoke and contrasts it with the yoke that is in the world. He invites the weary and heavy burdened to take His yoke which is easy and light, learn from Him and find rest. A believer takes on the yoke of Christ and learns from Him, His worldview, ways, moral framework, and purpose. An unbeliever takes on the yoke of the devil which by implication from Jesus's description, is heavy, burdensome, hard, stressful and leads to unrest. "For a Christian to enter into a partnership with an unbeliever is to court disaster. Unbelievers have opposite worldviews and morals, and business decisions made daily will reflect the worldview of one partner on the other. For the relationship to work, one or the other must abandon his moral center and move toward that of the other. More often than not, it is the believer who finds himself pressured to leave his Christian principles behind for the sake of profit and the growth of the business".

If a believer wearing the yoke of Christ enters into a business or other bond or relationship with an unbeliever wearing the yoke of the devil, they will have a tortured and hazardous relationship. No matter how respectful, sweet, or "loving" an unbelieving partner is, he is fundamentally at odds with Christ – he is in rebellion. "Therefore, those of us in Christ cannot be in a harmonious, God-pleasing relationship with an unbeliever. There is no fellowship between light and darkness (2 Cor. 7:14)! The Greek word for *"fellowship"* in this passage literally means *contact or intimacy*. Through Paul's inspired words, we learn that intimacy with unbelievers is not just discouraged – it's *impossible."*

To put it bluntly, going into business with an unbeliever is having the devil as your business partner! He has the right to come into your business, home, finances, career and life whenever and however he wants. Are you ready for that?

> *Being married to an unbeliever is having the devil as your father in law! Going into business with an unbeliever is having the devil as your business partner.*

CHAPTER 6
EMPOWERED

The next step to wholeness is power, God's power. The E in the WHOLE acrostic is for "Empowered". Empowered means to give someone the authority, right or power to be or do something. It means to authorize, license, commission, delegate, and qualify, someone. It also means to make someone stronger, and more confident, and in this sense, empowerment sets people free and enables them to be and accomplish all that they were created for.

> *For all who are led by the Spirit of God are the children of God.*

"Empowered" could mean almost anything in today's world, but for the Christian, it means only one thing, being filled with, and led by the Holy Spirit. Acts 1:8 states, "You will receive power when the Holy Spirit comes upon you." John 1:12 confirms, "But to all who believed Him and accepted Him, He gave the power to become children of God". And Romans 8:14 concludes, "For all who are led by the Spirit of God are children of God".

Who Is Holy Spirit?

He is the third person in the Godhead. He is one with the Father and the Son (1John 5:7). He is the Spirit of God, the Spirit of Christ, the divine empowerment, and the power of God. He is the energy force of the Godhead, the divine midwife that gives birth to the plans and purposes of God. He is the creative energy of God who hovered over the dark and empty earth in Genesis 1:2, to bring forth creation. The Holy Spirit is a person, with a mind, will and emotions.

He loves, (Romans 15:30, Romans 5:5, Galatians 5:22); has a will (1 Corinthians 12:11); has a mind, (Romans 8:27); and has thought, knowledge and understanding (1 Cor 2:10-13). The Holy Spirit has emotions, such as grief and sorrow (Ephesians 4:30); insult and outrage, (Hebrews 10:29); and can be lied to (Acts 5: 3-4).

Holy Spirit is the God and heavenly power source resident on the earth today. It is He who energizes the will of God, giving it life and substance. When the Bible says in Philippians 2:13, that "God is working in you, giving you the desire and the power to do what pleases him" it is talking about the Holy Spirit. He is the One who breathes God's life into any situation. The Hebrew word for the Holy Spirit is Ruach; and the Greek word is Pneuma. Both words mean "wind or breath". In Ezekiel 37, where the prophet saw a vision of the valley full of dry bones, even after the bones had joined together, and were covered with flesh, and had become a great army, they lay lifeless, until the prophet, at the direction of God, called forth the "Breath" of God (Ezekiel 37:9-10). The same thing happened in Genesis 2:7. After God formed man from the dust of the earth, he was lifeless until God breathed into him "the breath of life". Only then did man become a living person. Holy Spirit is the Breath of God. He brings the life of God into any situation or circumstance.

It is the work of the Holy Spirit to bring forth and give birth to the life and will of God. His role in our lives is to empower us to become like Christ, and live a victorious Christian life. This is why Jesus told His disciples to wait for the Holy Spirit. You cannot do anything of eternal consequence without the Holy Spirit. Indeed, you cannot live a successful Christian life without Him. And when He came in Acts 2:2, He came as "a rushing mighty wind".

The Role of the Holy Spirit

In John 14:26 Jesus said, "But the Helper, the Holy Spirit, whom the Father will send in My name, He will teach you all things, and bring to your remembrance all that I said to you." The Amplified version uses seven words to outline the role or job description of the Holy Spirit. He is the Comforter, Counselor, Helper, Intercessor, Advocate, Strengthener, and Standby. Since the work of the Holy Spirit is to help us to become more like Christ, His job description gives you an insight into what it is we are empowered to do.

The Holy Spirit represents Christ, and acts on His behalf. He seals or marks the believer with the favor, protection, ownership and authority of God, (Ephesians 1:13 -14, John 1:33, Acts 10:47-48), teaches believers, (John 14: 26), gives us power to be a witness for Christ (Acts 1:8), maintains fellowship with us, and facilitates our fellowship with the Father, (2 Cor 13:14); lives in our bodies as His temple, (1 Cor 6:19); helps us in our weaknesses - areas where we are prone to sin, failure, deficiency or inadequacy, (Romans 8:26); equips us for service, (Acts 6:3), guides us into all truth, (John 16:13); helps us administer the resources, plans, and agenda of God, (1 Corinthians 12:11); sanctifies us (Romans 15:16), leads us (Luke 4:1), spreads the love of God in our hearts (Romans 5:5), and so much more. Simply stated, we desperately need and cannot succeed without the ministry of the Holy Spirit!

Empowered to Be

The Holy Spirit empowers us to be. We live in a time and culture where there is an inordinate emphasis on doing. We are constantly inundated with activity, noise, and overstimulation. If you announce to your friends and coworkers that you are going on vacation, you are immediately bombarded with questions about what you are going to do? You can never just "be" on vacation. To many people, to just "be", is synonymous with boring and lonely. But that is not the truth of the scriptures. God is very invested in our being. He places our WHO above, and before our DO. He is completely committed to us being and becoming. That is the sum total of the empowering work of the Holy Spirit in our lives - to help us to be and to become. WHOLE Christians are men and women who are becoming through the power of the indwelling Holy Spirit.

Becoming Who You Are

In Genesis 1:26-27, God said:
> Let us make man in our image, according to our likeness and let them have dominion over the fish of the sea, and the birds of the air and over the cattle and over all of the earth and every creeping thing that creeps on the earth. God created man in his own image, in the image of God he created him. Male and female he created them.

"In Genesis 1, we see a pattern. When God wanted to create anything, he spoke to the source of the thing. In verse 11 God said: "Let the land sprout with vegetation. . .. And it was so." In verse 20

God said, "Let the waters swarm with fish and other life . . . and . . . Let the skies be filled with birds of every kind. . .. And it was so." In verse 24, God said, "Let the earth bring forth every sort of animal. . .. And it was so." The pattern is, God speaks to the source of the thing to be created to bring forth and it brought forth. When it came time to make man, God spoke to Himself. He said, "Let us make man in our image, according to our likeness." God is our source of origin, not tadpoles, a big bang, or anything else. Mankind came from God. We are His offspring (Acts 17:28).

God reproduced us after His kind—the god kind. He made us only just a little lower than Himself and delegated to us authority over all of creation (Psalm 8). "We are like God, having His attributes, nature and capable of manifesting His power. First John 4:17(b) states that as He, Jesus, is, so are we in this world. We are made in the image and likeness of Almighty God. An image is an authentic representation of a person or thing and likeness is the capacity to resemble, replicate, or reproduce that person or thing. We are an authentic representation of God in the earth and have the capacity to reproduce Him, His love, character, grace, and so forth on the earth" *(Godson)*. The work of the Holy Spirit is to help us to become who we are, sons and daughters of God.

Romans 8:29 states, "For God knew His people in advance, and He chose them to become like His Son, so that His Son would be the firstborn among many brothers and sisters". Jesus is the pattern son and the work of the Holy Spirit in our lives is to help us to become like Christ, and operate as sons and daughters of God in the earth. God our Father wants us to walk in the rights, authority and privileges of sonship. This was His express intent, plan, and purpose. He wanted us to occupy and rule over the earth, acting in His stead, as God. The mission of the Holy Spirit in our lives is to help us to understand the full meaning and implications of sonship, establish our destiny and birthright as sons and daughters of God, and empower us to walk in the privileges and rights of biblical sonship. The ultimate goal of God is to enable us to follow and reproduce the pattern—Jesus is the pattern Son. God wants every Christian to grow and mature from childhood into sonship until we look like Jesus in word and deed.

"Sonship is knowing your identity in Christ and walking in it! It means recognizing the nature, attributes, and capabilities of God within me until it moves me to act like God on the earth. As a "son" of God, *I AM* the spitting image of Christ: I look exactly like Jesus in my spirit. I simply need to believe it and allow what is already in my spirit to manifest through my soul and rule over my body" *(Godson)*.

A whole Christian in on a lifelong quest to become like Christ. We are "under construction", and the foreman is the Holy Spirit. This construction project will go on throughout our lifetime. Ruth Graham, the wife of world renowned evangelist Billy Graham died in 2007. The epitaph on her tombstone came from a road sign she once saw. It simply states, "end of construction – thank you for your patience". One day like Ruth, the end of construction will come for us when we see Jesus face to face, and know Him, even as we are known.

> *Whole Christians are men and women who are "becoming" through the power of the indwelling Holy Spirit.*

Empowered to Do

God has given us His Holy Spirit to empower us to do. Ephesians 2:10 states that, "we are God's masterpiece. He has created us anew in Christ Jesus, so we can do the things He planned for us long ago". As we submit to the "becoming" work of the Holy Spirit, we naturally begin to do. Becoming is an internal process, it is a heart affair. Becoming is critical because God focuses on the heart. He said in 1 Samuel 16:7, "man looks on the outward appearance, but the Lord looks at the heart". Becoming is the goal, but the key evidence, manifestation, or outworking of the becoming process, is the doing. God has things that "He planned for us" to do. Jeremiah 29:11 elaborates, "I know the plans I have for you says the Lord. They are plans for good and not for disaster, to give you a future and a hope". As we become, we are able to discern, recognize, and do His good plan and will. Philippians 2:13 sums it up: "For it is God who works in you both to will and to do His good pleasure"

The outward evidence of the inward working of God is that we begin to bear fruit. This is the purest evidence of the life of God in us, when we begin to naturally bear the fruit of God. You see, an orange tree can look like any other tree, but during fruit season, it will bring forth oranges, the distinctive fruit that marks, and sets it apart as an orange tree. In John 15:5, Jesus says, "I am the vine; you are the branches. Those who remain in me, and I in them, will produce much fruit. For apart from me you can do nothing". This is the litmus test, fruit! If we are truly becoming, then there will be the evidence of good fruit in our lives.

This means that you cannot authentically be a child of God without producing fruit that reflects the nature of God, and you cannot produce the god-kind fruit without the help, transformation, tutoring, agency, and partnership of the Holy Spirit. "That is why Jesus instructed the apostles to do nothing until they received the Holy Spirit. Wait for Him, Jesus said, because any work done without partnership with the Holy Spirit breaks the sonship mold. It is "strange fire"; fruitless work that will be burned up".

Galatians 5:22-23 describes the fruit that will showcase the life of God in us and the work of the Holy Spirit. It states, "But the Holy Spirit produces this kind of fruit in our lives: love, joy, peace, patience, kindness, goodness, faithfulness, gentleness, and self-control. There is no law against these things!" Note that this list of god-kind attributes is collectively called "fruit" and not "fruits". It is one fruit, a full complement, or portfolio of fruit produced by the Holy Spirit, and it comes as a package. This means that when we become children of God, we have the capacity to produce this entire package of fruit. We must not let the devil deceive us into an a la carte mindset, where we pick and choose which attributes to produce, or think that we are impotent to produce one or the other. I have heard people say how they can love and be kind and gentle, but cannot control themselves around sweets, or do not have patience. While that may be the fact, it is not the truth. The entire fruit package is deposited in us by the Holy Spirit, but like all other things in the word of God, it is in seed form. We need to cultivate the seed of self-control and patience to produce the fruit of self-control and patience in our lives. It is like a muscle that we develop through training and constant use (Hebrews 5:14).

The Holy Spirit also empowers us to do, through the distribution of His gifts. First Corinthians 12:4-10 lists nine gifts of the Holy Spirit. They are, word of wisdom, word of knowledge, faith, healings, miracles, prophecy, discerning of spirits, ability to speak in unknown languages, and the ability to interpret what is being said. Romans 12:6-8, lists other ministry gifts such as, prophecy, service, teaching, encouraging, giving, leadership ability and showing kindness. And Ephesians 4:11-12, lists the five-fold ministry gifts of apostles, prophets, teachers, evangelists and pastors, that Christ gave to build up the church.

The Bible is clear, everyone has a gift. The Holy Spirit makes sure of that. He alone decides which gift each person should have (1 Corinthians 12:11), and distributes them accordingly. Now, we must be careful. While the gifts are given by the Holy Spirit, they can sometimes be powered by charisma, momentum, sheer force of personality, natural talent, human applause, manipulation and so on. Also, they can be counterfeited by the devil and operate through demonic power (Acts 16:16-18). This is why, unlike fruit, gifts are not the telltale evidence of the life of God in us.

What is the Difference Between Gifts and Fruit?

1. Gifts can be counterfeited, but fruit cannot.

2. Gifts are outward demonstrations, but fruit is an inward transformation.

3. Gifts are manifested in, and are limited to this earth, but fruit is the nature of God, and endures eternally.

4. God's gifts and calling are irrevocable (Romans 11:29), so someone can walk away from God in their hearts, and still "manifest" the gifts of the Holy Spirit, but that is not the case with the fruit of the Holy Spirit. If you walk away from Him, you will wither, and will not bring forth any fruit (John 15:6).

5. You can display and manifest the gifts and go to hell (Matthew 7:21-23), but you cannot bring forth the fruit of the Holy Spirit and go to hell. This is because the word of God has enough power in itself to bring itself to pass. And, the name of Jesus is above every name, and at His name, every knee shall bow (Philippians 2:10). So, the fact that the word of God and the name of Jesus are used to manifest the gifts of the Holy Spirit, and perform miracles, is not an endorsement of the person using the Word or the name.

6. Gift is what we do, while fruit is how and why we do it. Ultimately, fruit is who we are and progressively become.

Empowered to Love

For the Christian who has been wounded in relationships, the Holy Spirit can empower you to love or love again. He specializes in healing broken hearts and lives. He can restore the broken places in your life, and empower you to dream again. With the Holy Spirit as your guide, you can love again. He can empower you to believe again, trust again, be vulnerable again, and love again, like you've never been hurt!

The work of the Holy Spirit is to build character, integrity, consistency, confidence, and security in the individual, as well as faith, and reliance on the finished works of Jesus Christ. These godly convictions are based on principles which are backed by the person, character, and power of God.

Holy Spirit Baptism

Have you received the Holy Spirit? The preceding discussion in this chapter makes the case for, and underscores the point that it is impossible to live a victorious Christian life without Him.

In Acts 19:2, apostle Paul asked believers in Ephesus the same question, and when they answered with a "No", he prayed for them and they were baptized in the Holy Spirit, and began to speak in other tongues or languages. God wants to do the same for you. Here is His promise:

> "These miracle signs will accompany those who believe: they will drive out demons in the power of my name. They will speak in tongues." (Mark 16:17).

> "In the last days,' God says, 'I will pour out my Spirit upon all people. Your sons and daughters will prophesy. Your young men will see visions, and your old men will dream dreams. In those days I will pour out my Spirit even on my servants— men and women alike— and they will prophesy" (Acts 2:17-18).

In 1 Corinthians 14:18, apostle Paul, who wrote a large part of the New Testament, said: "I speak in tongues more than you all."

You can receive this outpouring of the Holy Spirit in your life simply by asking God to baptize you with His Holy Spirit. This is when the Holy Spirit fills you up inside and you can speak in a new tongue or unknown language when you pray (Acts 2).

To receive the baptism of the Holy Spirit, pray this prayer:

Lord Jesus, you are the one who baptizes with the Holy Spirit. John the Baptist said, "I baptize you with water for repentance. But after me comes one who is more powerful than I, whose sandals I am not worthy to carry. He will baptize you with the Holy Spirit and fire" (Matthew 3:11). I ask you now to baptize me with your Holy Spirit - Amen! Now open your mouth and speak your new prayer language!

Note that you receive the person of the Holy Spirit the same way you received the gift of salvation - by faith. There are no fireworks, goose bumps, or magic feelings. Simply believe that you received the Holy Spirit when you asked in prayer, then open your mouth and speak - not in your native or learned language, but in the new language given to you by God. Keep in mind that God will not open your mouth for you and "make" you speak in tongues, just as He will not open your mouth for you and make you speak in English. You have to open your mouth and speak. Also, it is important to note that you will not understand what you are saying. So, the devil will tell you that you are making it up, that you are speaking gibberish, that it is fake, and that nothing happened. He is a liar and a thief. He wants to steal God's precious gift from you. Don't let him!

You may feel silly speaking a language you don't understand, but don't let that stop you. You are speaking to God spirit to spirit, and Romans 8:26 says that God understands exactly what the Holy Spirit is saying through your lips, because He prays for us according to the will of God. That is one of the many blessings of praying in tongues. Every time you pray in the Holy Spirit, your mind does not interfere and limit your prayers. So, you are praying directly and fervently according to the perfect will of God every single time!

If you've learned any human language, you know that you do not become proficient overnight. Just like any other language, your proficiency in your new prayer language will grow with practice. So, continue to speak in your new language every time you pray, and see the power of God unleashed in your life!

AFTERWORD

God wants every Christian to be whole, and to live a life filled with His presence, purpose, passion and power. But so many people live with a fragmented soul, areas of the soul that have been vandalized by the devil through toxic relationships, life circumstances, wrong thinking, and different kinds of bondage. God wants to heal and restore these broken areas of our lives. He wants to take our ashes and give us His beauty.

This book outlines five practical steps to wholeness in spirit, soul, and body. There is no wholeness without wellness, health, passion for God, love, and the Holy Spirit. These are five truths that frame the portrait of an abundant life, a life that is free from oppression, in the spirit, soul, and body. This book includes prayers to break free from different types of bondage, soul ties, and demonic oppression. God wants you to be whole and free. This book shows you how.

This book is based on decades of living successfully and prosperously as a W.H.O.L.E Christian woman. My prayer is that you will read this book and apply its truths to every area of your life. I pray that it will help you, and millions of God's people to be made whole and walk in the glorious liberty of the people of God. If you have not received Jesus as your Lord and savior, I urge and encourage you to pray the following prayer:

Lord Jesus, I believe in you. Come into my heart. I make you my Lord and Savior. Fill me with Holy Spirit. Thank you for giving me power and victory over sin, my flesh, the devil, and the world, Amen.

ACKNOWLEDGMENTS

1. Every book is the result of the work of a team, and this book is no exception.
2. Thank you to my friend and partner the Holy Spirit, at whose persistent nudging I finally wrote this book.
3. Thanks to my children, Emmanuel, Timothy and Rhema, whose support, encouragement and love kept me motivated.
4. Thanks to my family and friends who provided their thoughts and feedback on this book.
5. I am deeply grateful to God my Father, for His grace that has kept me sexually pure, and for the privilege of writing this book.
6. This book is a joint effort by many. I am truly grateful for the opportunity to partner with you all. I am better because of you.

NOTES

CHAPTER 1: WHOLENESS

1. Merriam Webster's Dictionary
2. Choosing A Life of Victory, Gloria Godson, Xulon Press, 2019.
3. On Death and Dying, Elizabeth Kubler Ross

CHAPTER 2: WELL

1. Nothing, Mick Inkpen, Hodder Children's Books
2. Let's Stop Comparing Ourselves: 6 Ways Jealousy is Stealing Your Self Love & How to Stop It, Aabye-Gayle, August 30, 2018.
3. Comparison is not the Thief of Joy, Abigail Dodds, March 26, 2018.
4. 10 Health Problems Related to Stress That You Can Fix, R Morgan Griffin, WebMD.
5. The Biblical Illustrator, Electronic Database, D Roberts, D. D., 2011.

CHAPTER 3: HEALTH

1. The World Health Organization's Definition of Health: Social Versus Spiritual Health, James S Larson, March 15, 1996.

2. The Spiritual Dimension: its importance to patients' health, well-being and quality of life and its implications for nursing practice, Ross L. International Journal of Nursing Studies, Volume 32, Issue 5, October 1995.
3. What is Spiritual Health? – Definition & Examples, Online Course, Study.com.
4. Healing the Soul of a Woman, Joyce Meyer, Faith Words, 2018.
5. Mental health: a state of well-being, World Health Organization, August 2014.
6. Why is Mental Health So Difficult to Define? Christopher Lane Ph.D., June 2016.
7. Mental Health: Keeping Your Emotional Health, Article, familydoctor.org.
8. 7 Signs of Emotional Wellness, Dr. Shannon Kolakowski, October 2013.
9. The Searing of the Christian Conscience, Steve Gallagher, January 2016.
10. C. H. Spurgeon, The Biblical Illustrator, Electronic Database. Copyright © 2002, 2003, 2006, 2011 by Biblesoft, Inc.
11. Amazing Facts About the Human Eye, Key -Whitman Eye Center, Blog, July.
12. The Holiness of God, John McArthur, Grace to You, Code GTY100.

13. Holiness of God – God's Attributes, All About God.com.
14. Top 5 Health-Related Components of Fitness, Tyler Read, November 23, 2017.
15. (Stillness and Rest: An Essential Part of Health, Dr. Deborah Anderson, Huffpost, January 28, 2016)
16. How to Keep a Positive Attitude When You Don't Feel Like It, Blog, Dr. Alan Zimmerman, July 11, 2017.
17. The Value of Human Suffering by Wayne Jackson, ChristianCourier.Com.

CHAPTER 4: ON-FIRE

1. The Zeal Of The Lord, A Sermon Published on November 12, 1914, Delivered by C. H. Spurgeon.
2. What is a Eunuch in the Bible, Got Questions, Your Questions, Biblical Answers, gotquestions.org.
3. Choosing a Life of Victory, Gloria Godson, Xulon Press 2019.

CHAPTER 5: LOVING

1. Zavada, Jack. "4 Types of Love in the Bible." Learn Religions, Apr. 17, 2019, learnreligions.com/types-of-love-in-the-bible-700177.
2. Are You A Narcissist? The Common Signs & Symptoms of Narcissistic Personality Disorder, Katherine George, June 7th, 2018.

3. Spirit Controlled Temperament, Dr. Tim LaHaye, Tyndale House Publishers 1993.
4. Know Yourself? 6 Specific Ways to Know Who You Are, Meg Selig Changepower, Article, Psychology Today, March 9, 2016.
5. The Samaritan Schism, Schisms in Jewish History: Part 2, Lawrence H Schiffman, Article, Bible History Daily, August 11, 2014.
6. Fatal Attractions, Jack Hayford, Regal Books, 2004.
7. 6 Ways to "Be Holy for I am Holy", Aretha Grant, Article, 1Believe.com
8. What Does it mean to be unequally yoked? GotQuestions.org.
9. Why Being Unequally Yoked Is More Dangerous Than You Think, Phylicia Masonheimer, Crosswalk.com Blog, February 22, 2017.

CHAPTER 5: EMPOWERED

1. Choosing A Life Of Victory, Gloria Godson, Xulon Press, 2019.

OTHER BOOKS BY THE AUTHOR

1. *Reclaim Your Destiny,* 31 Day Proclamations to Build Christ Esteem And Godly Self Image, *LifeWork Press,* 2022.

2. The Colt Story, LifeWork Press, 2021.

3. I AM The God Kind, Living in the Reality of Your Identity in Christ, LifeWork Press, 2021.

4. Fight to Win with Prayer and Proclamations, Grivante Press, 2020.

5. Single and Happy, Are You A W.H.O.L.E Single? Xulon Press 2019.

6. Choosing a Life of Victory, Xulon Press 2019.

7. Single and Happy, Are You A W.H.O.L.E Single? Study Guide.

8. Workbook: 5 Practical Steps to Wholeness in Spirit, Soul, and Body.

AUTHOR MINISTRY RESOURCES

LIFEWORK MINISTRIES, INC.
LifeWork Ministries empowers people to live the abundant life in Christ. We preach, write, and witness! Our compelling mission is to release the Life of Christ into the world by using our faith, thinking our faith, speaking our faith, singing our faith, praying our faith and sharing our faith. Connect with us on our website: **www.lifeworkministries.org** or send us an email at **lifeworkministriesinc@gmail.com**

WEEKLY RADIO BROADCAST
Gloria has a weekly Bible teaching program on REACH Gospel Radio and the Wilkins Radio network. You can hear her radio broadcast in cities across America. For the schedule of her weekly radio bible teaching program, please go to our website: **www.lifeworkministries.org.**

LICENSED CLINICAL PASTORAL COUNSELOR & TEMPERAMENT COUNSELOR
At LifeWork Ministries, we provide individual, family, marriage, pre-marital, relationship, career, ministry, and teen counseling. Contact us on our website at **www.lifeworkministries.org**

iDECLARE PRAYER AND PROCLAMATION
Gloria hosts the iDECLARE Prayer and Proclamation event. The word of God, spoken in faith, is the most powerful weapon known to man. At iDECLARE, we load, cock, and fire the word of God to transform our lives, families, and nations!

RACIAL EQUITY & UNITY
Gloria leads the Biblical Equity and Unity (BEU) collaborative, hosts the monthly BEU Community dialogue and the annual Racial Equity and Unity luncheon. Our vision is to educate, engage, and advocate on issues of biblical equity and unity; and to promote racial reconciliation and healing. Facebook@REUofDE.

SAVED SINGLES SUMMIT

Gloria hosts the Saved Singles Summit, a premier Christ-centered forum, which brings together Christian singles from churches across America for a time of fun, fellowship, empowerment, kingdom connections and new opportunities. Join us at: **www.savedsinglessummit.com**. Facebook@savedsinglessummit.

SINGLE CHRISTIANS CONNECT MEETUP GROUPS

For clean, fun, weekly activities and social events.
https://www.meetup.com/single-christians-connect/
https://www.meetup.com/philadelphia_single_Christians-connect/

SINGLE SENSE CONVERSATIONS

Monthly fun, interactive, Zoom panel discussion on singles issues, every 4th Friday.

THE GRACETALK

Weekly internet talk show hosted by Gloria on Sundays at 6pm:
https://www.facebook.com/TheGraceTalk/live_videos/

ABOUT THE AUTHOR

Gloria Godson is a multi-faceted corporate executive, with an illustrious career in the Energy Industry. She is a visionary, thought and strategy leader, and consummate senior executive. An attorney by training, she rose through several executive leadership positions to become a Vice President in Exelon Corporation, the largest energy company in America.

Most importantly, Gloria is a Christian leader, Bible teacher, author, prayer minister, and conference speaker. She is a Licensed Clinical Pastoral Counselor, Certified Temperament Counselor and Professional Clinical Member of the National Christian Counselors Association. She is the CEO of LifeWork Ministries, and has a weekly Bible teaching radio program. She hosts Wholeness Workshops, Temperament Workshops, the premier annual Saved Singles Summit, the iDECLARE Prayer and Proclamation event, the Racial Equity and Unity Community Events, and the live *GraceTalk* internet talk show.

Gloria served on the Board of Word of Life (WOL) Christian Center in Newark, Delaware, a full gospel, non-denominational church, for over twelve years. And for over fifteen years, Gloria also served as overseer of the WOL prayer ministries, and is a regular eye witness to God's miraculous answers to prayer. She is a powerful minister of the word of God, with a singular focus on building lives and the kingdom of God. She is a dynamic speaker who connects with both professional and Christian audiences across the country and around the world.

Gloria loves to serve her community! She is on the Board of Faith and Freedom Coalition Mid-Atlantic. Gloria is an online missionary with Global Media Outreach, a dedicated volunteer with the REACH community outreach, the Sunday Breakfast Mission, Urban Promise, Exceptional Care for Children, and more. She loves God passionately and believes in the unstoppable power of Almighty God to do the impossible. She has three children and lives in Delaware, United States.

AUTHOR CONTACT

To invite Gloria to speak, send her your prayer request, place a book order, or simply connect, please go to:

www.lifeworkministries.org

www.gloriagodson.com

Facebook@TheGraceTalk

Instagram@TheGraceTalk

YouTube@TheGraceTalk

LifeWork Ministries, Inc.

P. O. Box 56,

Townsend, DE 19734

www.lifeworkministries.org

EMAIL

lifeworkministriesinc@gmail.com

www.ingramcontent.com/pod-product-compliance
Lightning Source LLC
LaVergne TN
LVHW040140080526
838202LV00042B/2968